SCHOLASTIC

SCHOLASTIC Go Grammar

Course Book

Level 8

The following pieces have been used with permission or are in public domain:
Page 5: "Detective Baradacharan" from *Funny and Funnier* by Shireshendu Mukhopodhyay, trans. Palash Baran Pal and Abhijit Gupta
Page 24: *The Importance of Being Earnest, A Trivial Comedy for Serious People* by Oscar Wilde
Page 28: "Makes the Whole World Kin" by O. Henry
Page 77: "Dinosaurs and After" from *Why We Are Where We Are: A Brief History of the Universe* by Swagata Deb and Supriya Seshadri
Page 78 and 82: *The Five Senses: A Reference Guide* by Leslee Lazar
Page 80: "Black Holes" from *103 Scientific Principles, Ideas, Theories and Stuff* by Shobit Mahajan
Page 86: "The Dare of Death" from *Spooky Stories* by Adit Marawala
Page 108: "Chicago" by Charles Sandburg
Page 112 and 118: "Piranhas" and "A Kind of Love Song" from *The Fried Frog and other Funny Freaky Foodie Feisty Poems* by Sampurna Chattarji
Page 114: *Harsha Vardhana* by Devika Rangachari

Published by Scholastic India Pvt. Ltd.
A subsidiary of Scholastic Inc., New York, 10012 (USA)
Publishers since 1920, with international operations in Canada, Australia,
New Zealand, the United Kingdom, India, and Hong Kong.

For information regarding permission, write to:
Scholastic India Pvt. Ltd.
A-27, Ground Floor, Bharti Sigma Centre
Infocity-1, Sector 34, Gurgaon (Haryana) 122001
Email: education@scholastic.co.in

Series editor: Vivek Gopal
Illustrations: Rituparna Sarkar
Layout design and typesetting: Mansi Bansal

First edition: 2010
Reprinted: 2010, 2011 (thrice), 2012 (twice), 2014 (twice), 2016 (twice), 2018 (twice), 2019

ISBN-13: 978-81-8477-510-5

Contents

Topic	Lesson/Work sheet	Page
Introduction		4
Nouns	Work sheets 1–2	5
Pronouns	Work sheets 3–4	7
Adjectives	Work sheets 5–6	9
Adverbs	Work sheets 7–8	11
Conjunctions	Work sheets 9–10	13
Prepositions	Work sheets 11–12	15
Clauses	Work sheets 13–18	17
Transitional Words and Phrases	Work sheet 19	23
Direct and Indirect Speech	Work sheet 20	24
Sentences	Work sheet 21	27
Articles	Work sheet 22	28
Infinitives	Lesson 1	29
	Work sheets 23–24	31
Verbs	Lesson 2	33
	Work sheets 25–28	35
Modifiers	Lesson 3	39
	Work sheets 29–30	42
Comma Splices and Run-on Sentences	Lesson 4	44
	Work sheets 31–33	45
Similes and Metaphors	Lesson 5	48
	Work sheets 34–38	50
Clichés	Lesson 6	55
	Work sheet 39	56
Oxymorons	Lesson 7	57
	Work sheet 40	58
Revision 1		60
Mechanics of Writing	Lesson 8	67
	Work sheets 41–44	70
Quoting, Paraphrasing and Block Quotations	Lesson 9	74
	Work sheets 45–46	77
Summary Writing	Lesson 10	79
	Work sheet 47	82
Essay Writing 1	Lesson 11	83
	Work sheets 48–50	86
Essay Writing 2	Lesson 12	92
Book Review	Lesson 13	94
	Work sheet 51	98
Movie Review	Lesson 14	100
	Work sheets 52–53	102
E-mail Writing	Lesson 15	105
	Work sheet 54	107
Revision 2		108
Word Banks		120
Evaluation Sheet		131

Introduction

Being aware of grammar rules enable us to communicate efficiently, clearly and understandably. As human beings, we can put sentences together even as children—we can all *do* grammar. But to be able to talk about how sentences are built, about the types of words and word groups that make up sentences—that is *knowing* about grammar. And *knowing* about grammar offers a window into the human mind and into our amazingly complex culture.

Scholastic Go Grammar 6, 7 and *8* are a series of English grammar course books for the middle-school reader. These books have been created to provide a holistic approach to grammar and language usage that is geared towards practical application over rote memorisation. Simply put, *Scholastic Go Grammar* is a fun approach to grammar that is both instructive and edifying.

The *Scholastic Go Grammar* books

1. Include lesson plans that cover the written and spoken rules of grammar. These include practical solutions for problems that concern even native speakers of English.
2. Have extensive work sheets that engage the student with the rules and exceptions of the English language through practical instances
3. Encourage revision of topics covered in earlier books with more advanced exercises.
4. Include essays, poems, speeches from the finest writers around the world, with an added emphasis on Indian writers. The follow-up comprehension sections dissect how grammar allows these writers to express themselves as well as they do.
5. Incorporate activities that centre around community building in the classroom and events from the student's lives.
6. Provide an exhaustive compilation of supplemental material that is referential and provide a checklist of common writing errors.
7. Follow the current NCERT curriculum and pedagogical principles.
8. Enable educators to monitor students' progress over the course of a lesson through 'free writing' exercises and evaluation sheets provided.

An informative and motivating set of books, *Scholastic Go Grammar* will help students apply the rules of grammar in spoken and written English to make them effective and articulate communicators.

Nouns

Abstract nouns are those words that indicate intangible things like sensation or emotion.

I Complete the sequence with the correct irregular plural nouns.

1	one foot	two ________	**2**	a phenomenon	a few ________
3	a mouse	several ________	**4**	a tooth	a few ________
5	my sister-in-law	my ________	**6**	a fish	three ________
7	a leaf	many ________	**8**	a louse	many ________
9	my wife	their ________	**10**	an ox	a herd of ________

II In the following passage, circle all the common nouns, proper nouns, concrete nouns, abstract nouns, countable and uncountable nouns, and list them in the table below.

Detective Baradacharan was a very clever man no doubt, but his behaviour was somewhat weird. He never did what ordinary people did. When entering someone's house, he rarely used the front gate. He preferred to enter by climbing the boundary wall at the back of the house, or by scaling the rainwater pipes to the roof, or in some such strange way. If he wanted to go to Mogra, he would get on a mail train. He knew fully well that mail trains do not stop at Mogra. And yet that was what he would do, and jump out of the moving train at Mogra. In blazing sunshine, he was seen wearing a raincoat and a pair of high boots. It was not easy to understand why he sometimes wore overcoats in summer. He was a master at donning disguises. And because he was in disguise all the time, people forgot what he actually looked like.

Countable	Uncountable	Common	Proper	Concrete	Abstract

Nouns

We use possessive nouns to show ownership. The possessive noun always appears before the object being modified.

I In the following sentences, the possessive nouns are missing apostrophes. Rewrite them correctly.

1 My neighbours dog eats irresponsibly.

____

2 My grandfather lives in the childrens room at the back of the house.

____

3 Why is your dog running away with Charles trousers?

____

4 Which team won last years World Cup?

____

5 Someone stole all the buses seats last night.

____

6 I enjoy Shakespeares sonnets; I read them at least once a year.

____

7 This newspaper said that tonights concert has been cancelled.

____

8 My cars tyres are missing.

____

9 Monkeys frequently visit my fathers garden to enjoy a midnight snack.

____

10 We watched our neighbours puppy chew my sisters slipper.

____

Pronouns

Pronouns are used to replace a noun or another pronoun.

I Fill in the blanks with suitable personal pronouns.

1 Does ____________ know that ____________ was absent today?

2 Please tell ____________ that ____________ had called.

3 Please don't tell ____________ about ____________ .

4 ____________ can't float because ____________ has no buoyancy.

5 I remember ____________ . They bought the house from ____________ .

II Fill in the blanks with suitable reflexive pronouns.

1 He gave ____________ a treat for being right.

2 They bickered amongst ____________ for ages.

3 We enjoyed ____________ at the park.

4 The dog is scratching ____________ .

5 Since she lives alone, she cooks for ____________ .

6 The mountaineers prepared ____________ for the trip.

7 I had to force ____________ to drink the bitter medicine.

8 Please, don't trouble ____________ about it.

9 Do ____________ a favour and buy new trousers.

10 The clumsy cat picked ____________ off the floor.

Pronouns

We use relative pronouns when the object of a sentence is the same as the subject.

I Join together the following pairs of sentences using relative pronouns.

1 I met a man. He had no shoes.

____

2 I got onto a train. It was crowded.

____

3 They were very happy. They won the game.

____

4 You bought a book. Show me the book.

____

5 The boys arrived late. They missed the movie.

____

6 I am going to talk to the girl. She is sitting in front.

____

7 You gave me this movie. It is terrible.

____

8 The car was parked in front of the bank. It was stolen.

____

9 We stayed in a hotel. The hotel had no windows.

____

10 That's the boy. His mother is a writer.

____

Adjectives

A possessive adjective acts like a possessive pronoun but unlike a pronoun it modifies a noun.

I Complete the sentences with possessive adjectives.

1 He's from Portugal. ______________ name's Djalmo.

2 They're married. ______________ children's names are Nitu and Smitu.

3 We're related. ______________ mothers are cousins.

4 She's eight. ______________ brother's nine.

5 I'm British. ______________ name's Boris.

6 You're late. ______________ books are in the classroom.

7 I have a sister. ______________ name is Pooja.

8 The dogs love to play in ______________ garden.

9 Their children are on ______________ vacation.

10 ______________ company builds cannons.

11 Aishwarya and I have class together. ______________ teacher is Ms Payal.

12 Wait, ______________ cat is this?

13 The monkey is licking ______________ paw.

14 My calculator is broken; can I use ______________?

15 After living alone for many years, she moved back to ______________ parent's house.

Adjectives

Adjectives identify or quantify words by providing more information about them.

I Use the appropriate adjectives to complete the sentences.

1 Ameet showed a lack of concern for the driver of the ____________ taxi involved in the accident.

2 Finishing school is the ____________ option you have.

3 Where are my ____________ toys?

4 Thomas Pynchon writes ____________ books that few people understand.

5 Dad said he would allow me to stay up late only after I am ____________ years old.

6 I have been feeling ____________ lately and have not felt like doing anything.

7 The brave knight took a trip to slay the ____________ dragon in the other world.

8 The storm brought ____________ conditions to the area.

9 I have several hours of ____________ dance practice ahead.

10 The bear loomed ____________ over us.

11 They found a ____________ goldfish floating belly up in the bowl.

12 Do you know if ____________ sneakers are Bimaldeep's?

13 Inspite of being young and successful, Sudip somtimes makes ____________ decisions.

14 I decided to order food once I caught the ____________ smells emanating from the kitchen.

15 He might look ____________ but he is really trustworthy.

Adverbs

An adverb modifies a verb, clause, adjective or adverb to indicate manner, time, place and cause.
Adverbial clauses do the work of an adverb. They can tell how, when, where or why an action takes place. They begin with a conjunction.

I Rewrite the following sentences using adverbial clauses.

1 Dennis finished reading the book. Then he went to bed.

____

2 The policemen delayed the drivers. The roads were cleared.

____

3 The rains had caused mudslides. The roads were not safe to drive on.

____

4 Joe studies hard. He wants to become a doctor.

____

5 Wait. We will fix your computer.

____

6 I was eating. I choked on a bone.

____

7 Bhuvan finished his homework. Then he ate an apple.

____

8 Tejasvini donates her suits to charity. She has outgrown them.

____

9 Aditya built roller coasters for a living. He started studying law.

____

10 I enjoyed travelling. I was much younger.

____

Adverbs

Adjectives modify nouns. Adverbs modify verbs, adjectives and other adverbs.

I In each of the following pairs, indicate whether the highlighted word is an adverb or an adjective.

1 My bus for school arrived **late**, as usual. ____________

I caught the **late** train to Jalandar. ____________

2 The exam was **harder** than I thought. ____________

I must try **harder** next time. ____________

3 You have to give it your **best**. ____________

This is some of my **best** work. ____________

4 Suchitra blogs about her life **daily**. ____________

The milkman's **daily** caterwaul drives me insane! ____________

5 If you drive **fast** enough, we might just make it on time. ____________

Pinky loves **fast** cars. ____________

6 We are **low** on supplies. ____________

The helicopter flew **low** over the trees. ____________

7 I hope you are doing **well**. ____________

I did **well** on my exam. ____________

8 She is **sure** about her answer. ____________

Surely, you're joking? ____________

WORK SHEET 9

Conjunctions

A conjunction is a word that is used to connect sentences or clauses. Subordinate conjunctions indicate chronology, cause, effect, opposition and position.

I Join the pair of sentences using a conjunction.

1 We can go for a walk. We will do so if the weather is fine.

____

2 We had better pack now. We may not have time to catch our flight.

____

3 School was called off. There was an outbreak of the flu.

____

4 Priya has been sick. She has been so since last week.

____

5 Do not start the music yet. The speaker has not finished.

____

6 The winning team was very happy. They were declared the champions.

____

7 The players gave their best. They still lost.

____

8 Kim has no time to eat breakfast. She is late.

____

9 I took my umbrella. It was raining.

____

10 You should stay away from bears. They are dangerous.

____

Conjunctions

Correlative conjunctions join sentences of equal importance.

I Fill in the blanks with the correct correlative conjunctions.

1 ______________ my sister ______________ her husband live in San Diego.

2 Her cat doesn't shed ______________ much ______________ your mangy cat.

3 Maybe I should take ______________ maths ______________ science instead of humanities.

4 ______________ ______________ did Vivek lose his iPod, ______________ he ______________ had his car stolen.

5 ______________ Roger ______________ Humbert know how to change a flat tyre.

6 I don't like science classes. I want to take ______________ biology ______________ chemistry.

7 You will ______________ have to take the bus ______________ walk to school today.

8 Depending on her budget, my sister is going to ______________ Chennai ______________ Delhi this winter.

9 My cousin would like to take a vacation as well. He cannot decide ______________ to go to Dubai ______________ Cambodia.

10 The show was ______________ entertaining ______________ educational.

11 She ______________ ______________ wrote the play ______________ also directed it.

12 This is the last question. You are now finished with ______________ this exercise ______________ this section.

WORK SHEET 11

Prepositions

A preposition is a word which shows relationships among other words in the sentence.

I Fill in the blanks with the correct prepositions.

1 I was ____________ the boat.

2 We are going to go ____________ the movies tonight.

3 His e-mail implies that he is out ____________ the country.

4 I was waiting ____________ the corner ____________ the road.

5 I arrive at work ____________ 9:00 am every day.

6 I don't know the name of the person who sits ____________ me.

7 The car broke down ____________ the bridge.

8 You forgot to paste stamps ____________ the envelope.

9 Watch ____________ for that cyclist!

10 I'd like to speak ____________ the manager, please.

11 The puppy has managed to get ____________ the fridge.

12 We were driving ____________ work when we hit the cow.

13 I've been waiting for the doctor ____________ noon.

14 I didn't want to go ____________ the mall.

Prepositions

We use **at** for a precise time, **in** for months, years, longer periods, and **on** for days and dates.

I Fill in the blanks with the correct prepositions of time.

1 Jay is going to work ____________ a Saturday.

2 My birthday is ____________ March.

3 To be more specific, my birthday is ____________ 25 March.

4 I have been waiting for the train ____________ two hours.

5 Don't worry, I'll have this finished ____________ Friday.

6 My flight is ____________ Friday, ____________ noon.

7 I began work on my magnum opus ____________ 1985.

8 Don't be ridiculous; there were no dinosaurs ____________ the seventeenth century.

9 I fell asleep ____________ the play.

10 Hurry up! The movie starts ____________ a few minutes.

11 No one has heard from him ____________ last month.

12 We have to finish our project ____________ this week.

13 The play is running ____________ August ____________ October.

14 This book was first published ____________ 1965.

15 I'm going to be in Kerala ____________ a week.

WORK SHEET 13

Clauses

A subordinate or dependent clause cannot stand alone as a sentence.

I Each sentence has a clause in bold letters. Identify whether it is a subordinate clause or principal clause.

1 If you don't fix the car, **it will continue to give you trouble.** ____________

2 **While the car is at the mechanic's,** I am taking the bus. ____________

3 You don't have to work all night **if you have worked a little each day.** ____________

4 Before you leave for the airport, **you will want to rest.** ____________

5 I can't go out with you **since I don't have any money.** ____________

6 **Whether he makes it or not**, I still need to leave. ____________

7 **I will turn down the music** when you go to sleep. ____________

8 **Since you've been studying all week**, you can take a day off to rest. ____________

9 Until he apologises to me, **I will not see him.** ____________

10 I took my umbrella **because it looked like it might rain.** ____________

11 You should turn the work in now; **however, the teacher won't review it till later.** ____________

12 **She will visit us** if she can. ____________

WORK SHEET 14

Clauses

Adjectival clauses, also called relative clauses, do the work of adjectives and tell us more about people and things.

I Choose the correct adjectival clause to complete the following sentences.

1 Vivek is the boy __________ shaved his head. He is completely bald now.

a who *b* that *c* which

2 The food __________ she is eating looks healthy.

a who *b* that *c* whose

3 A dishwasher is a machine __________ washes dishes.

a who *b* that *c* who's

4 Is the bat the only mammal __________ can fly?

a who *b* who's *c* that

5 Look! That's the actor __________ mother is from my city.

a who *b* whose *c* who's

6 I don't like dogs __________ are bigger than me.

a who *b* whose *c* that

7 I felt bad for the girl __________ fell down the stairs.

a who *b* that *c* who's

8 Jasmine is a flower __________ is white and very fragrant.

a who *b* whose *c* that

9 They are cheering the girl __________ birthday it is.

a who *b* whose *c* who's

10 There's the author __________ book you liked so much.

a who *b* whose *c* who's

WORK SHEET 15

Clauses

An adjectival clause describes a noun or pronoun in one of the other clauses in a sentence. Adjectival clauses begin with a relative pronoun—who, whom, whose, which, that.

I Combine each of the following pairs of simple sentences into one complex sentence containing an adjectival clause.

1 The theft was committed last night. The police have caught the man.

2 French is derived from Latin. Latin was once spoken throughout Europe.

3 You are looking sad. Can you tell me why?

4 He had several plans for making money quickly. All of them have failed.

5 The wrestler was proud of his strength. He despised the weakness of the clowns.

6 This is the village. I was born here.

7 You put the keys somewhere. Show me the place.

8 Paul was an old gentleman. He was my travelling companion.

9 A fox once met a crane. The fox had never seen a crane before.

10 The shopkeeper keeps his money in a wooden box. This is the wooden box.

Clauses

Adverbial clauses answer questions about the verb that relate to time, location, purpose and condition.

I Circle the adverbial clauses in the following sentences.

1 The lettuce is wilted because it was in the car for too long.

2 Since I got my glasses, I can see what I am reading.

3 Although Rajat works hard, his boss rarely rewards him.

4 Whenever I go to the mall, I have a hard time remembering why I went.

5 No one may leave the area until the police have checked all the buildings.

6 After we returned from trekking, I took a nap.

7 Having never driven before, I was not very good.

8 Since I have never been there, I brought a map.

9 We didn't eat because the restaurant was closed.

10 Although Barnabas broke the vase, he did not feel guilty about it.

11 If we continue burning fossil fuels, the temperature of the earth will rise.

12 She took a management course so that she could get a better-paying job.

13 I'm not going unless he comes along.

14 I can't do anything without their knowing about it.

Clauses

A subordinate clause is linked to the principal clause by a conjunction or a relative pronoun.

I Choose the correct subordinate clause to complete the following sentences.

1 Gulls are sometimes called "rats of the air" ________________ they will eat almost anything.

a which *b* since *c* but *d* that

2 Usually a bird species gains public recognition ________________ faces the danger of extinction.

a which only *b* only when it

c only when *d* which only it

3 It ________________ the *Titanic* sank while crossing the Atlantic.

a is 1919 when *b* in 1912 that

c which was in 1912 *d* was in 1912 that

4 Christopher Columbus, a famous Italian navigator, ________________ until recently considered to be the first European to sail to the New World.

a has *b* was

c who has been *d* that was

5 Many people are careless ________________ their garbage.

a when recycling *b* the recycle

c recycling about *d* about recycling

6 Many early nomadic inventions ________________ important to the agricultural community.

a were *b* being

c that were very *d* very

WORK SHEET 18

Clauses

A subordinate clause must be attached to a main clause to give the sentence meaning.

I Choose the correct subordinate clause to complete the following sentences.

1 A lunar eclipse ________________ the earth passes between the sun and the moon, causing the earth to become dark.

a occurs *b* which occurs

c that occurs *d* occurs when

2 Dry cleaning is a process in which the first step ________________ a garment in a clearing solution.

a involves soaking *b* involving

c that soaks *d* which involves

3 A farmer's almanac ________________ contains much information, including details about the yearly movements of the sun and the moon.

a which *b* a book which

c is which *d* is a book that

4 Romany is a language ________________ gypsies speak.

a that *b* and which

c which is of *d* is that which

5 ________________ Constance burped, the other students in the room turned to see who had done it.

a When *b* If

c Since *d* Even

Transitional Words and Phrases

Transitional words and phrases show the association between thoughts, sentences or paragraphs and they help make writing smoother.

I Choose the most suitable transitional words or phrases given in brackets that fit both the meaning and the punctuation given.

Anti-comic Bigotry in the Educational Establishment

One of the more controversial topics at the recent International Summit of Textbook Makers and Grammarians was the inclusion of more comic books in the school syllabus. ______________ (If/Since/Just as) happier work environments have been found to lead to better productivity, the use of educational materials that children can enjoy enhances their ability to learn. When presented with an attractive format, children are far more willing to absorb the information it contains. ______________ (Furthermore/ On the other hand/But), comics, combining as they do both visual and written elements, are an exceptionally efficient way of presenting a lot of information in a small amount of space. ______________ (Consequently/So/Actually), one would assume that the academic establishment would welcome textbooks in a comic book format. ______________ (For instance/However/Since), this has not been the case. ______________ (On the contrary/As a consequence/Whereas) the students have embraced the idea of learning from comic books, their teachers have not been as quick to take to these new books. ______________ (Besides/In fact/Instead), the reaction has been positively hostile, with a number of prominent teachers stigmatising the books as "lightweight" and their adoption as a "dumbing down" of the standards of education.

Direct and Indirect Speech

Indirect speech (also called reported speech) is used to communicate the gist of what some one said but without using the exact words. The tenses of the verbs are changed and quote marks are not used.

I Given below is an extract from a play. Read it and answer the questions that follow.

Jack. I have lost both my parents.

Lady Bracknell. To lose one parent, Mr Worthing, may be regarded as a misfortune; to lose both looks like carelessness. Who was your father? He was evidently a man of some wealth. Was he born in what the Radical papers call the purple of commerce, or did he rise from the ranks of the aristocracy?

Jack. I am afraid I really don't know. The fact is, Lady Bracknell, I said I had lost my parents. It would be nearer the truth to say that my parents seem to have lost me ... I don't actually know who I am by birth. I was ... well, I was found.

Lady Bracknell. Found!

Jack. The late Mr Thomas Cardew, an old gentleman of a very charitable and kindly disposition, found me, and gave me the name of Worthing, because he happened to have a first-class ticket for Worthing in his pocket at the time. Worthing is a place in Sussex. It is a seaside resort.

Lady Bracknell. Where did the charitable gentleman who had a first-class ticket for this seaside resort find you?

Jack. [*Gravely.*] In a handbag.

Lady Bracknell. A handbag?

Jack. [*Very seriously.*] Yes, Lady Bracknell. I was in a handbag—a somewhat large, black leather handbag, with handles to it—an ordinary handbag, in fact.

Lady Bracknell. In what locality did this Mr James or Thomas Cardew come across this ordinary handbag?

Jack. In the cloakroom at Victoria Station. It was given to him in mistake for his own.

Lady Bracknell. The cloakroom at Victoria Station?

Jack. Yes. The Brighton line.

Lady Bracknell. The line is immaterial. Mr Worthing, I confess I feel somewhat bewildered by what you have just told me. To be born, or at any rate bred, in a handbag, whether it had

Direct and Indirect Speech

Spoken words in direct speech are separated from unspoken words by a comma, a question or an exclamation mark.

handles or not, seems to me to display a contempt for the ordinary decencies of family life that reminds one of the worst excesses of the French Revolution. And I presume you know what that unfortunate movement led to? As for the particular locality in which the handbag was found, a cloakroom at a railway station might serve to conceal a social indiscretion—has probably, indeed, been used for that purpose before now—but it could hardly be regarded as an assured basis for a recognised position in good society.

Jack. May I ask you then what you would advise me to do? I need hardly say I would do anything in the world to ensure Gwendolen's happiness.

Lady Bracknell. I would strongly advise you, Mr Worthing, to try and acquire some relations as soon as possible, and to make a definite effort to produce at any rate one parent, of either sex, before the season is quite over.

Jack. Well, I don't see how I could possibly manage to do that. I can produce the handbag at any moment. It is in my dressing room at home. I really think that should satisfy you, Lady Bracknell.

II **Rewrite the conversation in indirect or reported speech. Avoid the question-and-answer format.**

____

____

____

____

____

____

____

____

____

Direct and Indirect Speech

The fist spoken word in direct speech begins with a capital letter.
For example: Neeraj muttered, "No one ever listens to me."

Sentences

A simple sentence contains a subject and a verb, and it expresses a complete thought. A compound sentence contains two independent clauses joined by a coordinator. A complex sentence has an principal clause joined by one or more subordinate clauses.

I Identify the following sentences as simple, complex, compound or compound-complex.

1 The most popular sport in India is cricket. __________

2 Ancient China and Japan had a form of football, and even Rome had a game that resembled football. __________

3 In the Middle Ages, whole towns would gather to play community sports. __________

4 Posts were built at opposite ends of many towns, and hundreds of people who lived in those towns would play on each side. __________

5 Such gatherings resembled full-scale brawls. __________

6 The first side to reach the opposite post were declared champions. __________

7 Both sides had many wounded players, and they couldn't play again for a whole year. __________

8 Roman baths were somewhat similar to modern gyms, although they had little equipment for exercising. __________

9 Ancient Rome alone had 856 baths; most of them were private. __________

10 Citizens who became rich were expected to build baths for their fellow citizens, and many generously built huge marble facilities. __________

11 For the equivalent of about a rupee, any Roman citizen could be massaged, scrubbed and soaked in a public bath. __________

12 A Swedish bath often involves exercise, and a hot, dry room to sweat. __________

13 Next, bathers visit a hot, steamy room, and the final stage is a plunge into ice-cold water. __________

14 After the bathers finished their baths, they would wrap themselves in towels and walk vigorously around the area. __________

15 Though Priya prefers watching romantic films, she saw the new action movie, and she enjoyed it a lot. __________

16 Some contestants also sat around and played chess and checkers in game rooms. __________

Articles

We don't use articles with professions.
For example: He'll probably go into medicine.

I Insert articles in the appropriate places in the following passage.

house was residence. By its boarded front door and untrimmed Boston ivy burglar knew that mistress of it was sitting on some oceanside piazza telling sympathetic man in yachting cap that no had ever understood her sensitive, lonely heart. He knew by the light in third-storey front window, and by lateness of the season, that master of house had come home, and would soon extinguish his light and retire. For it was September of year and of soul, in which season the house's good man comes to consider roof gardens and stenographers as vanities, and to desire return of his mate and more durable blessings of decorum and moral tendencies.

II Fill in the blanks with suitable articles.

1 I want to buy ____________ laptop computer soon.

2 Can you go to ____________ shop and buy some milk?

3 We have to be at ____________ station in ____________ hour.

4 This is ____________ exciting match.

5 He has to take ____________ university exam next week.

6 If you're not busy, do you want to watch ____________ movie with me?

7 I need to go on ____________ holiday.

8 Where has all ____________ pudding gone?

9 He has ____________ honorary degree.

10 Can I ask you ____________ question?

11 He broke ____________ glass while washing up.

12 ____________ Tropic of Cancer crosses Taiwan.

Infinitives

An infinitive is the base form of a verb with **to.**

- to run, to play, to cry, to yell, to jump

Infinitives can be used as nouns, adjectives or adverbs.

- To sleep is the only thing I want after studying all night for my test.

To sleep functions as a noun because it is the subject of the sentence.

An infinitive will almost always begin with **to.** However, an infinitive will lose its **to** when it precedes certain verbs such as feel, hear, let, make, see and watch.

- Can you make me a sandwich?
- Can you hear the drums, Fernando?

The pattern looks like this:

special verb + direct object + infinitive - *to*

- As soon as Thor felt the rain splatter on his hot, dusty skin, he knew that it was time to end the battle.

felt = special verb; rain = direct object; splatter = infinitive minus the **to.**

- I was shocked when I saw my sister mount the unicorn, a frightening beast with one horn and rainbow tresses.

saw = special verb; my sister = direct object; mount = infinitive minus the **to.**

When trying to decide between using an infinitive or the **ing** form of the verb, pay attention to the role of time in the statement.

- The children like **to go** to the zoo.
- The children like **going** to the zoo.

In the above statements, the meaning is identical. However, **going** is a general statement implying that the children typically enjoy the complete experience of visiting a zoo. **To go** implies that children

Infinitives

enjoy going to the zoo and does not say anything about their complete experience. In certain instances, the difference in meaning caused by an infinitive or an **ing** verb can be considerable.

➔ I stopped **to eat a samosa.**

➔ I stopped **eating samosas.**

The first sentence indicates that the speaker stopped an activity, to eat a samosa. The second statement states that the speaker does not eat samosas any more.

Split Infinitives

An infinitive is considered 'split' when a word is placed between **to** and the infinitive verb.

➔ **To boldly go** where no one has gone before.

Some writers believe that splitting an infinitive is the greatest crime of our generation. Others, however, consider the split infinitive an acceptable construction, in informal writing.

➔ I hope **to quickly finish** my homework.

When deciding to split an infinitive, consider your audience. If the piece of writing is formal, avoid splitting; if you feel it adds to the desired tone and voice of your writing, split.

Infinitives

Infinitives can be used as nouns, adjectives or adverbs.

I Join together the following sentences using infinitives.

1 He did not have a single penny on him. He could not buy a loaf of bread.

2 The mugger carried a knife. He intended to frighten the poor tourist.

3 He speaks the truth. He is not afraid of it.

4 He wants to be famous. He works hard for that reason.

5 They have six children. They must provide for all of them.

6 Everyone should do his duty. The army expects this of every soldier.

7 She quit the job. She wanted to climb mountains.

8 He collects toy cars. It is his hobby.

9 Byron awoke one morning. He found himself famous.

10 The boy was happy. He survived the stampede.

11 The rodeo clown was relieved. The enraged bull spared him.

12 I carry an umbrella. It protects me from rain.

Infinitives

An infinitive will almost always begin with **to**. An infinitive loses the **to** when it precedes verbs like **feel**, **hear**, **bet**, **make**, **see** and **watch**.

I Fill in the blanks with the correct form of the words given in the brackets.

1 Authorities have recently instituted a toll for ____________ (drive) on highways.

2 They hoped ____________ (reduce) the number of vehicles on the road.

3 Motorists have to choose between ____________ (pay) the toll or not ____________ (driving) on the highway.

4 The toll has been successful in ____________ (divert) local traffic away from highways.

5 As vehicles on the road reduce, journey time into cities tends ____________ (decrease).

6 According to a poll, only a few people say it is okay ____________ (charge) people for ____________ (drive) into cities.

7 They are happy ____________ (find) traffic ____________ (flow) more easily.

8 Before ____________ (charge) the toll fee, the average speed into cities was around 20 kmph.

9 Motorists who choose ____________ (pay) the toll can ____________ (drive) at greater speeds.

10 Public transport has seen a marked ____________ (rise) in passengers as a result.

11 That this policy has already begun ____________ (impact) the environment is abundantly clear.

12 Hopefully, this initiative will ____________ (reduce) our carbon footprint.

Verbs

Moods

Mood is a term we use to show how a process (verb) is used in a sentence.

Verb moods indicate the attitude towards what is being discussed. Identifying the moods of the helps us gauge the tone of the piece.

A verb may be in one of four **moods.**

The Indicative Mood

The **indicative mood** is the most common and is used to express facts and opinions. Most of the statements you make or read are in the indicative mood.

- Joe picks up the boxes.
- The dog attacked the postman.
- Charles fell out of the window.

The Imperative Mood

The **imperative mood** is used to give orders.

- Pick up those boxes.
- Attack.
- Close the window.

When paired with "please" or "could", it can also be used to indicate requests.

- Please pick up those boxes.
- Please close the window.
- Could you pick up those boxes?

The Subjunctive Mood

The **subjunctive mood** is used to express hopes, wishes or uncertainty. It does not appear very often in everyday conversation or writing, and is used in a set of specific circumstances.

Verbs

The subjunctive is found in a handful of traditional statements. For example, in the sentence **God save the Queen**, the verb **save** is in the subjunctive mood. Similarly, in **Heaven forbid**, the verb **forbid** is in the subjunctive mood.

- I wish Joe would pick up those boxes.
- I hope that dog didn't attack the postman.
- If only that window had been closed.

We can also use the **conditional** auxiliary verbs **could**, **should** or **would** to express the same mood.

- I wish he was kinder to me. (subjunctive)
- I wish he would be kinder to me. (conditional)

The Infinitive Mood

The **infinitive mood** expresses an action or state without reference to any subject. They include participle forms ending in **ed** and **ing.** Verbs in the infinitive mood are not used as verbs, but as other parts of speech.

- To err is human; to forgive, divine.

Here, **to err** and **to forgive** are used as nouns.

- He is a man to be admired.

Here, **to be admired** is an adjective, the equivalent of **admirable.** It describes the noun **man.**

- He came to see you.

To see you is used as an adverb to explain why he came.

WORK SHEET 25

Verbs

The imperative mood is used to give commands.

I Identify the sentences as indicative, imperative, subjunctive or infinitive.

1 Take the books to her room. ______________

2 If only we had filled petrol at the last stop. ______________

3 He does really enjoy playing cricket. ______________

4 I hope we are able to see a movie tomorrow. ______________

5 Please collect all the plates from the table. ______________

6 What is going on here? ______________

7 She is a child to beware of. ______________

8 She wishes her father were here. ______________

9 My bank manager is incompetent. ______________

10 If you were rich, we wouldn't be in this mess. ______________

11 This is all your fault. ______________

12 Hercule tripped down the stairs. ______________

13 I wish I didn't have to eat this. ______________

14 That is a fine goal to aspire to. ______________

Verbs

The subjective mood expresses doubt or something contrary to fact.

I Fill in the blanks with the correct form of the verbs.

1 If Garima ______________ here now, we could ask her opinion. (to be)

2 We would have forgotten our tickets last night if she ______________ not ______________ us. (to remind)

3 ______________ I ______________ earlier, I would have arrived on time for the wedding. (to leave)

4 Would you travel next summer if you ______________ enough money? (to have)

5 If it ______________ yesterday, we would not need to water the lawn. (to rain)

6 If he ______________ you last Wednesday, he would have asked your help. (to see)

7 If they ______________ to leave now, they would need to hurry up. (to want)

8 ______________ they ______________ of the concert yesterday, they would have wanted to go. (to know)

9 Would you not have stayed longer if you ______________ able to? (to be)

10 If you ______________ the package tomorrow, they would only receive it in two weeks. (to mail)

11 If he ______________ the book now, he would enjoy it. (to read)

12 If we ______________ more attention yesterday, we would know what the test is on. (to pay)

Verbs

The indicative mood is used to express facts and opinions or to make inquiries.

I Rewrite the following passage in the indicative mood.

When I was a little boy, I always wished that my father was rich. I wanted my family to live in a huge mansion. We could have had several pets and huge tracts of land for them to run on. I hoped that my father would buy us horses, and that we would spend our holidays abroad. I wanted us to live in a big city because I always thought that our small town was boring and I would have liked us to have been able to go to fancy restaurants, cinema and shops.

Verbs

The subjunctive verb expresses hopes, wishes or uncertainty.

I Choose the correct subjunctive verb forms to complete the following sentences.

1 If he ______________ not injured, we would have won the match.

a would have been *b* was *c* were

2 The teacher wishes that her students ______________ more motivated.

a were *b* was *c* would be

3 My music teacher asks if we ______________ twice a day.

a would practice *b* practiced *c* practice

4 The club requires that each member ______________ his dues.

a paid *b* had paid *c* pays

5 We wished that we ______________ the rival team.

a beat *b* had beaten *c* would have beaten

6 I would have caught the ball if I ______________ closer to it.

a had been *b* was *c* were

7 The rules state that each tenant ______________ responsible for his pets.

a be *b* is *c* was

8 I realised that if I ______________ to improve, I would need to spend several weeks practicing.

a was *b* were *c* would

9 To avoid injury, stunt men ______________ on the proper way to fall down.

a were focussed *b* focussed *c* focus

10 "Do you surf?" "No, but I wish I ______________."

a can *b* could *c* were

Modifiers

Modifiers are words, phrases or clauses that provide description in sentences. Modifiers breathe life into sentences.

Take a look at this sentence:

➜ Vivek dropped his phone.

Now read what several well-placed modifiers can do:

➜ Poor Vivek, who just wanted to make a quick call to order a tasty pizza, dropped his phone on the cement surface, gagging with disgust as a cockroach wiggled out of his school bag, a sight requiring months of therapy before Vivek could open that bag again.

Modifiers can be adjectives, adjectival clauses, adverbs, adverbial clauses or absolute phrases, infinitive phrases, participle phrases and prepositional phrases.

Absolute phrase	modifies a subordinate clause. It may precede, follow or interrupt the principal clause.
Participle phrase	does the work of an adjective. It begins with a past or present participle.
Infinitive phrase	begins with an infinitive and can function as a noun, adjective or adverb.
Adverbial phrase	describes a verb. It does the work of an adverb.
Prepositional phrase	modifies nouns and verbs while indicating the various relationships between them.

Modifiers

The example on the previous page contains at least one example of each:

Adjective = poor

Adjective clause = who just wanted to make a quick call

Adverb clause = cockroach wiggled out of his school bag

Absolute phrase = a sight requiring months of therapy before Vivek could open that bag again

Infinitive phrase = to order a tasty pizza

Participle phrase = gagging with disgust

Prepositional phrase = on the cement surface

You have a certain amount of freedom in deciding where to place your modifiers in a sentence:

- The hippo chased the boat vigorously.
- The hippo vigorously chased the boat.
- Vigorously, the hippo chased the boat.

Modifiers describe other words, making the meaning of those other words more specific. Modifiers answer the following questions about the words they modify:

What kind? Which one(s)? How many or how much? Whose?

When? Where? Why? How? To what extent? Under what conditions?

Watch this sentence become more specific as modifiers are added:

Basic sentence: Editors earn salaries.

(How many editors?) Many editors earn salaries.

(Which editors?) Many editors in educational publishing earn salaries.

(What kind of salaries?) Many editors in educational publishing earn poor salaries.

(When?) Many editors in educational publishing earn poor salaries forever.

However, you must be careful to avoid misplaced or dangling modifiers—modifiers that are positioned so that they appear to modify the wrong thing.

Modifiers

Dangling Modifiers

A dangling modifier occurs when the modifier seems to be associated with the wrong word or phrase.

➩ Having been thrown in the air, the dog caught the stick.

This sounds as if the dog had been thrown in the air. The correct form would be:

➩ The dog caught the stick that had been thrown in the air.

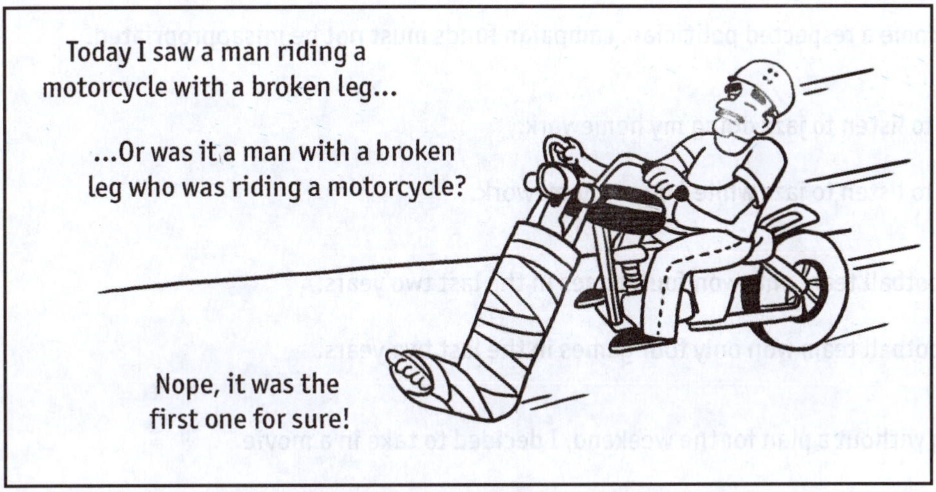

➩ Being in a dilapidated state, I was able to afford the car.

This sentence sounds like the speaker was in a dilapidated condition. It should read:

➩ I was able to afford the car because it was in a dilapidated state.

Modifiers

A modifier can be an adjective, an adverb or a clause acting as an adjective or adverb that adds information to another element in the sentence.

I Tick the correct sentence in each pair.

1 Spending way too much money on his old cat, Fred's salary just wasn't enough. ☐

Spending way too much money on his old cat, Fred soon found he'd used up his salary. ☐

2 To become a respected politician, one must not misappropriate campaign funds. ☐

To become a respected politician, campaign funds must not be misappropriated. ☐

3 I like to listen to jazz doing my homework. ☐

I like to listen to jazz while I do my homework. ☐

4 The football team only won four games in the last two years. ☐

The football team won only four games in the last two years. ☐

5 Being without a plan for the weekend, I decided to take in a movie. ☐

Being without a plan for the weekend, a movie seemed a good idea at the time. ☐

6 The cemetery, where famous composers, artists and writers are buried, is open daily, except on Thursdays. ☐

You are welcome to visit the cemetery where famous composers, artists and writers are buried daily, except on Thursdays. ☐

Modifiers

A dangling modifier is a word or phrase that modifies a word not clearly stated in the sentence.

I The following sentences have dangling modifiers. Correct them by attaching an object or person for the modifier to modify or rearrange the sentence structure.

1 Disappointed that vacation would soon end, September came all too quickly.

---

2 He went to the library wearing a leather jacket.

---

3 After reading the paper, the telephone rang.

---

4 Working all afternoon, the foundation was completed.

---

5 Laughing loudly, the joke pleased the audience.

---

6 Forgetting to fill petrol, the scooter wouldn't start.

---

7 Writing slowly, the exam seemed endless.

---

8 Celebrating my success, a party with my friends lasted till midnight.

---

9 Not seeing the pothole, the pedestrian went tumbling.

---

10 My friend went on and on, describing the details of her wedding in the elevator.

Comma Splices and Run-on Sentences

If there are two subjects and two verbs in a sentence, you have to separate them to clarify meaning. When two sentences are joined with no connecting punctuation, it's called a **run-on sentence.**

➾ This medicine **may prevent** heartburn it **may cause** diarrhoea

There are three easy ways to correct a sentence like this.

- Create two separate sentences.

➾ This medicine **may prevent** heartburn. It **may cause** diarrhoea.

- Use a semicolon.

➾ This medicine **may prevent** heartburn; it **may cause** diarrhoea.

- Use a comma and a coordinating conjunction (typically, **and**, **but** or **or**).

➾ This medicine **may prevent** heartburn, but it **may cause** diarrhoea.

You cannot simply use a comma to separate two complete sentences. This is called a **comma splice.**

A comma splice is the use of a comma to join two principal clauses instead of a conjunction, semicolon or full stop.

➾ I came, I saw, I conquered.

➾ This medicine **may prevent** heartburn, it **may cause** diarrhoea.

Do not use a comma if there is only one subject.

➾ This medicine **may prevent** heartburn but **cause** diarrhoea.

In this example, the noun phrase **this medicine** serves as the subject for the entire sentence.

Comma Splices and Run-on Sentences

A comma splice occurs when two independent clauses are joined by a comma but without a coordinator.

I Decide if the sentence is a comma splice or a complete sentence. In case of a comma splice, rewrite the sentence correctly.

1 Joy is always late for work, nobody seems to care. ☐ comma splice ☐ complete sentence

___

2 Cool weather is nice, cold temperatures are dangerous for some people. ☐ comma splice ☐ complete sentence

___

3 Vani broke her ankle on the weekend; now she is in a great deal of pain. ☐ comma splice ☐ complete sentence

___

4 Driving a car is fast and comfortable, riding the bicycle is better for one's health. ☐ comma splice ☐ complete sentence

___

5 When a student likes his class, he is more likely to put more effort into his work. ☐ comma splice ☐ complete sentence

___

6 Justin has an interview with the UN, I might get a job as his assistant. ☐ comma splice ☐ complete sentence

___

7 After I was paid last week, I was able to eat proper food. ☐ comma splice ☐ complete sentence

___

Comma Splices and Run-on Sentences

You can also change one of the clauses into a subordinate clause to avoid a splice.

I Decide if the sentence is a comma splice or a complete sentence. In case of a comma splice, rewrite the sentence correctly.

1 Due to the fact that I am so busy this week, I don't have time for my pets. ☐ comma splice ☐ complete sentence

____

2 Whenever Meena does not sleep enough, she gets a horrible headache. ☐ comma splice ☐ complete sentence

____

3 The air conditioner is too loud, my cat Cleo is louder. ☐ comma splice ☐ complete sentence

____

4 I got up late this morning, I didn't have time for breakfast. ☐ comma splice ☐ complete sentence

____

5 It's raining outside, grab an umbrella. ☐ comma splice ☐ complete sentence

____

6 The cat jumped from step to step, it landed gracefully after each jump. ☐ comma splice ☐ complete sentence

____

7 I learnt those songs on the guitar, I simply chose not to play them. ☐ comma splice ☐ complete sentence

____

Comma Splices and Run-on Sentences

If the independent clauses are very short, then a comma splice is acceptable. For example: You've been to Dubai, haven't you?

I The following sentences all contain a comma splice. Rewrite them correctly.

1 The team valiantly ran down the field, still they could not score a goal.

2 Even though the year is almost over, the teacher does not know my name, she often confuses me with other students.

3 I think that the teacher has been grading me unfairly, all she does is look for mistakes.

4 While time often erases bad memories, my wife never forgets anything, she even remembers things that happened over a decade ago.

5 Advanced classes at the university level are now being taken by many school students, some schools even offer them special programmes.

6 After the sixth wicket, I went home, my friends stayed.

7 One person had been exporting farm animals, in fact he exports over 3,000 cows a year.

8 All over the country, people sell junk over the internet, these people are making profits.

9 My father is chairman of the Committee on Foreign Relations, he also heads the Society for No Hierarchies.

10 Entrepreneurship involves the study of small businesses, college students are embracing it enthusiastically.

Similes and Metaphors

Similes and metaphors compare dissimilar objects that have one or more attributes in common.

A simile makes this comparison explicit by using words like **as** or **like**.

The comparison in a metaphor is not as explicit as in a simile. Instead, a metaphor juxtaposes the objects being compared or their attributes so that the reader may deduce the similarity.

Writers use similes and metaphors to explain things, to express emotion, and to make their writing more vivid and entertaining. Discovering fresh similes to use in your own writing also means discovering new ways of looking at your subjects.

Similes often use irony or sarcasm. In such instances, they might even mean the opposite of the adjective used:

- His explanation was **as clear as mud**. (Not clear at all since mud is ... well, mud.)
- The movie was **like watching paint dry**. (Long and boring.)

We come across similes and metaphors every day. They are often found in poetry and other literature and even music:

- Death has many times invited me: it was like the salt invisible in the waves—Pablo Neruda
- Happy as pigs in mud—David Eddings

Similes and Metaphors

- As idle as a painted ship upon a painted ocean—Samuel Taylor Coleridge
- Jubilant as a flag unfurled—Dorothy Parker
- A woman needs a man like a fish needs a bicycle—U2
- Like a rolling stone—Bob Dylan
- You are as subtle as a brick to the small of my back—Taking Back Sunday

Allusions

Allusions are literary devices that evoke associations, and extra information in the reader's mind with only a word or a reference. It relies on the reader being able to understand the allusion and being familiar with the meaning hidden behind the words.

➪ Amit didn't like to spend money. He was no Scrooge, but he spent on anything except the bare necessities.

Did you spot the allusion to Scrooge? That name should bring to mind an image of someone who 'pinches pennies' and hoards money. But the allusion only works if the reader is familiar with Charles Dickens' novel, *A Christmas Carol*.

Similes and Metaphors

A metaphor is a brief comparison that talks about one thing as if it were another. The comparison is implied.

I Create a metaphoric statement by combining "__________" of "__________."

The first blank is usually a concrete noun (something tangible) and the second an abstract noun (an idea or an emotion).

1 Start with: a teacup of ____________________. Write a list of abstract nouns to fill the second blank. Two have been done for you.

a a teacup of wit   a teacup of __________   a teacup of __________

b a teacup of joy   a teacup of __________   a teacup of __________

2 Take the abstract nouns you have used (*joy*, *wit*, etc.) and for each, list three concrete nouns to fill in the first blank.

a __________ of joy   __________ of __________

b __________ of joy   __________ of __________

c __________ of joy   __________ of __________

Notice that changing one part of the metaphor changes the entire metaphor. A *teacup of wit* is different from a *garden of wit*.

This is practice but it's also play. When you practice, you generate ideas. You experiment with the language, putting words together in ways you otherwise wouldn't. You end up writing poems.

3 Write three versions of each of the following.

a a pocket of __________   a pocket of __________

b a cyclone of __________   a cyclone of __________

c a forest of __________   a forest of __________

d a brick of __________   a brick of __________

e a library of __________   a library of __________

4 Use one of the metaphors developed through the exercise to write a poem. Share it in class.

Similes and Metaphors

Similes often employ sarcasm or irony by making obviously contradictory statements.

I Identify whether each sentence contains a simile or a metaphor. Write what is being compared to what.

1 The burglar was as agile as a three-legged cat. ☐ simile ☐ metaphor

____

2 Chemistry is as clear as mud. ☐ simile ☐ metaphor

____

3 The policeman's steps were thunder as he ran after me. ☐ simile ☐ metaphor

____

4 Strength and dignity are her clothing. ☐ simile ☐ metaphor

____

5 My teacher has a heart of stone. ☐ simile ☐ metaphor

____

6 Love is like being beaten by a sock filled with loose change. ☐ simile ☐ metaphor

____

7 No one invited Kareem to parties because he's as much fun as a broken umbrella. ☐ simile ☐ metaphor

____

8 The bar of soap was a slippery eel during my little brother's bath. ☐ simile ☐ metaphor

____

9 The kids in the playground moved as if on fire. ☐ simile ☐ metaphor

____

10 Their food tastes like mud cooked in more mud. ☐ simile ☐ metaphor

____

Similes and Metaphors

Unlike a metaphor, a simile uses the words **like**, **as** or **as if** to indicate that a comparison will follow.

I Finish each sentence with whatever metaphor or simile comes immediately to mind.

1 Paint spilled on the floor like ______________________.

2 A spider under the rug is like ______________________.

3 The graffiti on the abandoned building was like ______________________.

4 Nothing was the same, now that it was ______________________.

5 The water gushed out of the dam like ______________________.

6 A child in ______________________ is like a ______________________ in ______________________.

7 ______________________ is like muscles stretched taut over bone.

8 Vineet drank water as if ______________________.

9 The security guard walks along the lobby as if ______________________.

10 Music is my ______________________.

Similes and Metaphors

A metaphor can be seen as an understanding of one concept in terms of another.

I Identify the word or phrase that is being described by each simile.

1 David said, "I believe that smoking is like playing with fire."

____

2 Homer walked along the beach and listened to the ocean. His sadness was as unending as the waves.

____

3 Don't tell Sheetal that her soup tastes like boiled socks.

____

4 Nikhil waited impatiently for his older brother to calm down. "I think you're acting like a baby," he said.

____

5 Louise was offended when I said that she was as flaky as a snowstorm.

____

6 The floor is as slippery as greased glass when it rains.

____

7 E.T. was not comfortable about his situation. He felt like a bug sitting under a magnifying glass.

____

8 Our lack of practice would indicate that our performance will last as long as a balloon in a roomful of kittens.

____

9 Englebert said, "It's been a hard day's night, and I've been working like a dog", quoting the Beatles.

____

10 This suitcase is as light as a feather. I hope you are carrying all the books.

____

Similes and Metaphors

Similes and metaphors often use the seemingly unrelatable aspects of two nouns to create a vivid and jarring affect.

I For each statement, create a simile or a metaphor that helps to explain the statement and make it more vivid.

1 Aishwarya has been working as a chimney sweep for six days a week, ten hours a day, for the past twelve years.
(*Use a simile or a metaphor to show how worn out Aishwarya was feeling.*)

____

____

2 Raju had been working all day in the blazing sun.
(*Use a simile or a metaphor to show how hot and tired Raju was feeling.*)

____

____

3 This is Snoodgrass' first day at school and he is in the middle of a chaotic morning.
(*Use a simile or a metaphor to show either how confused Snoodgrass feels or how chaotic the morning is.*)

____

____

4 Harold spent his entire summer vacation watching cartoons and soap operas on television.
(*Use a simile or a metaphor to describe the state of Harold's mind by the end of his vacation.*)

____

____

5 After all the troubles of the past few weeks, Payal felt peaceful at last.
(*Use a simile or a metaphor to describe how peaceful or relieved Payal was feeling.*)

____

____

LESSON 6

Clichés

A cliché is an expression or idea that has been overused to the point of losing its original meaning or effect.

- Time is money.
- Once upon a time...
- All's fair in love and war.

A cliché can also refer to an idea that has come to have a meaning different from its literal meaning. The phrase **sweaty palms** has come to mean more than the fact that one's palms are sweaty. When we say someone has sweaty palms, it is understood to mean "he is nervous" because the expression has become a cliché.

Using clichés in speech is a common occurrence. Using clichés in writing is ill-advised as reading a tired cliché can't give your reader a fresh sensory detail. The mind dulls when reading a tired, ineffective comparison and we tend to skim over the words without thinking about the meaning.

You don't have to avoid clichés like the plague, but you risk boring your readers if you don't. Observe the following.

- George **hit the nail on the head** with that remark.

Can become

- George was timely and accurate with that remark.

The second sentence may not be as poetic as the first, but it conveys the impact that George's remark made better.

Clichés

A cliché is a phrase or opinion that is overused and betrays a lack of original thought.

I The following paragraph contains a number of clichés. Underline the clichés used.

In this day and age, good teachers are few and far between. My deepest, darkest secret is my desire to be one of those teachers—one that is worth her weight in gold, who works her fingers to the bone, hand in hand with students to prepare them to meet the trials and tribulations of life. I was walking on air as I arrived at my first class, until I realised I'd forgotten my room number. A wave of optimism washed over me when I saw a classroom door open. I sauntered up to the door, when BANG, like a bolt from the blue, one of my new students—later proven to be rotten to the core—darted out and slammed the door right in my face. My anxiety grew by leaps and bounds, when, as luck would have it, a fellow teacher came by and consoled me. I gathered my wits about me and opened the door. I could sense the undercurrent of excitement as I walked into the room and the guilty student beat a hasty retreat to his seat. Anxious for my reaction, he breathed a sigh of relief when I decided not to make a tempest in a teapot about the incident. Cool as a cucumber, I posed question for the ages, "The writing process is neither writing nor a process. Discuss." In their youthful glee, all the students jumped on the bandwagon to discuss. Slowly but surely, the humiliating experience became as water under the bridge as I continued the uphill battle to become all that I can be as a teacher.

Oxymorons

An oxymoron is a figure of speech that places contradictory terms together. Writers often use an oxymoron to call attention to or to emphasise an apparent contradiction.

The best known oxymoron is perhaps from Shakespeare's *Romeo and Juliet* ,"Parting is such sweet sorrow." The juxtaposition of "sweet" and "sorrow" is an oxymoron, combining contradictory ideas of joy and pain. Parting is sorrowful, more so in the case of young lovers. Parting is pleasurable, presumably, because of the anticipation of getting to meet again.

Oxymorons are more commonly found than we might think.

- On the subject of terrorism, the US President said, "I want to move with all **deliberate haste.**"
- To excel as a businessman you must take **safe risks.**

Oxymorons can be useful when things have gone contrary to expectation, belief or desire. By pitting two seemingly contradictory words or phrases against each other, oxymorons affect a startling effect on the reader (the highs and lows created by opposing emotional responses).

- "Gob was always my **least favourite** son," said Lucille.
- When Abantika saw the length of the English exam, she let out a **silent scream.**

Oxymorons

An oxymoron is a figure of speech in which apparently contradictory terms appear in conjunction.

I The following poem is made entirely out of oxymorons. Underline the oxymorons.

Ladies and gentlemen, skinny and stout,
I'll tell you a tale I know nothing about;
The admission is free, so pay at the door,
Now pull up a chair and sit on the floor.

One fine day in the middle of the night,
Two dead boys got up to fight;
Back to back they faced each other,
Drew their swords and shot each other.

A blind man came to watch fair play,
A mute man came to shout "Hooray!"
A deaf policeman heard the noise and
Came to stop those two dead boys.

He lived on the corner in the middle of the block,
In a two-storey house on a vacant lot;
A man with no legs came walking by,
and kicked the lawman in his thigh.

Oxymorons

An oxymoron is often used to call attention to or to emphasise an apparent contradiction.

He crashed through a wall without making a sound,
into a dry creek bed and suddenly drowned;
The long black hearse came to cart him away,
But he ran for his life and is still gone today.

I watched from the corner of the big round table,
The only eyewitness to facts of my fable;
But if you doubt my lies are true,
Just ask the blind man who saw it.

Revision 1

I Circle the infinitive phrase in each sentence.

1 Because he loved French, Beckett refused to write in any other language.

2 The most important thing to do is not always the easiest.

3 To keep the road clear, they diverted pedestrian traffic.

4 Some of the students had questions to ask after class.

5 To do well at college, you should spend some time at the library.

6 Danish slowly reeled the fish in to keep it from escaping.

7 We finally found an actor to play the lead.

8 Why is Vinay attempting to eat forty-five dumplings at one go?

9 The salesperson changed his pitch to suit each potential buyer.

10 I have to do well in civics this year.

II Fill in the blanks with either the infinitive or the -ing form of the verb.

1 Can we ______________ them?

a trust *b* to trust *c* trusting

2 I'm glad ______________ you.

a see *b* to see *c* seeing

3 If at first you don't succeed, don't give up ______________ .

a try *b* to try *c* trying

4 I find it difficult _______________ her question.

a answer *b* to answer *c* answering

5 Shruti is fond of _______________ ice cream.

a eat *b* eating *c* to eat

6 You will _______________ famous one day.

a be *b* to be *c* being

7 I am not interested in _______________ chess.

a learning *b* to learn *c* learn

8 I am not allowed _______________ my car here.

a park *b* to park *c* parking

9 Toby is bad at _______________ coffee.

a making *b* to make *c* make

III Tick the sentences which use the correct verb tenses or moods. Rewrite the incorrect ones.

1 By the time we arrived, all the cakes had been eaten. ☐

____

2 They had planned to have bought a puppy, but they bought fish instead. ☐

____

3 After the road was cleared, we were able to drive through. ☐

____

Revision 1

4 Will, in Nick Hornby's *About a Boy*, is an idealist ill prepared for life in the real world. ☐

5 Call me tomorrow if you want to go biking. ☐

6 The hurricane tore up the trees, lifted them over the roof and deposited them onto the road. ☐

7 Most of the children brang their own instruments and sang many songs. ☐

8 I thought I seen him planting tulips behind the house. ☐

9 You are suppose to read the instructions before assembling the shelf. ☐

10 If I was you, I would avoid any mention of the subject. ☐

IV Rewrite the following sentences using a comma, a full stop and/or a conjunction.

1 Turkey is a lovely country it has lovely people and great food.

2 She gave me a stern glare I was really anxious.

3 She always drives everywhere she is really lazy.

4 Martha loves pie apple is her favourite kind.

5 The meal was a disaster he is useless in the kitchen.

6 Give me that package it's mine.

7 Parul left her job she could not stand her boss.

8 She opened the new bottle she had bought the previous summer.

9 Given his ineptitude in the kitchen the meal was surprising delicious.

10 Our solar system has nine major planets only one is known to have intelligent life.

V Tick the sentences that are correct. Rewrite the sentences that are comma splices.

1 My apartment is too small, I have no room for my books and television set. ☐

2 I'm exhausted, however, I will go to the party anyway. ☐

3 Vishal opened his freezer, then he noticed that two cartons of ice cream had melted. ☐

4 Although I understand the definition, comma splices still confuse me. ☐

5 A comma splice occurs when two complete sentences are joined only by a comma, I need to remember that rule. ☐

6 Our modern life is very easy, healthcare is better than it was fifty years ago. ☐

7 This street is full of fast-food restaurants, people eat there very often. ☐

8 I did not hear my alarm, I woke up forty minutes late. ☐

9 My dog is a constant companion, he sleeps on my bed. ☐

VI Rewrite the sentences that have a misplaced or dangling modifier.

1 Flashing a huge grin, Bart apologised for being late and then distributed sweets to the children.

2 The surgeon was able to quickly and painlessly re-attach Pinocchio's nose.

3 While driving yesterday, a tree began to fall towards Joginder's car.

4 Before buying a new house, you should carefully consider what you need and what you can afford.

____

5 After borrowing from all his friends, he had barely enough money for a cup of coffee.

____

6 My friend is starting a weight-loss programme in two days of five meals a week.

____

7 Having entered the theatre, the music seemed to overwhelm me.

____

8 Upon leaving the room, the lights began to flicker.

____

9 To eliminate the errors, the paper needs to be rewritten.

____

10 Carrying the packages to the car, my foot got stuck in a pot hole.

____

VII Read the following sentences and circle the principal clauses. Identify the subordinate clauses as adjectival, adverbial or noun clauses in the space provided.

1 There is the car that had been repaired because the wheel had broken off.

____

2 After you finish repairing the car, which you were shown, you will be paid.

____

3 That she had made a mistake became apparent when the wheel fell off.

4 Although he thinks he can dance, he can't.

5 Since my grandfather has high blood pressure, he has to watch what he eats.

6 If we had taken the train, we would not have arrived on time.

7 The milk that I bought yesterday is finished.

8 The police formed a barricade where the workers were striking.

9 Hamlet wanted to kill his uncle so that his father's murder would be avenged.

10 The grammar police are searching for the person who wrote the dangling modifier and the split infinitive.

Mechanics of Writing

Having mastered the parts of speech, it is important to turn our eye towards the mechanics of speech to examine the ways in which our word choices can push a narrative forward, create a scene or hint at unsaid context.

Participants

These are the *people*, *places*, *ideas* and *things* that take part in the action of a sentence.

- **The cranky old man** yelled at the children.

The actual participant is **man** but within the context of the sentence it is **cranky old man**, since this is what propels the action of the sentence forward.

- **Lots of monkeys** attacked the unsuspecting grammar editor.

In certain instances, participants are omitted when they are conventionally understood from the context of the situation.

Do you drive?	(a car)
Have you eaten yet?	(lunch/dinner)
Shall I pour?	(the tea/coffee)
My team has won.	(the match/race)
I can't see from here.	(the screen, the time, the board)

Some situations or events typically have no participants, especially those pertaining to the weather, time and distance.

- It's snowing.
- It's quarter to two.
- That's a long way from here.

In these cases, the pronoun refers to the subject that may appear to be out of our frame of reference but is culturally understood.

A participant can be words or a phrase that carries out the action or that is affected by it.

Mechanics of Writing

Processes

These are the *action* or *state of being* verbs.

Processes are best described as action verb groups.

- The artist **had been painting** the garage.
- The children **were not being** very quiet in the nursery.

There are three main types of processes:

Material processes are processes of 'doing' (kick, run, eat) or 'happening' (melt, fall, slip).

Mental processes or processes of 'experiencing' or 'sensing' (see, hear, feel, want, regret).

Relational processes, or processes of 'being' (be, seem) or 'becoming' (become, turn).

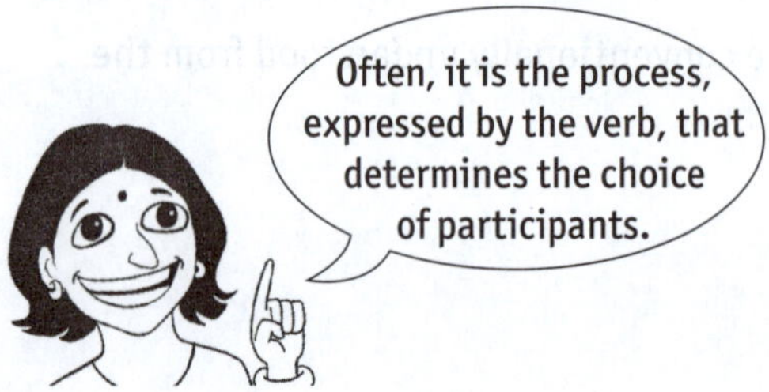

- "Where is the statue?"

The above sentence has no verb but the verb 'stand' is implied within the context of the statement . Similarly, in the question, "Do you drive?" the word being implied is 'a vehicle', even though we don't say it.

Attributes

These are words or phrases that add to the meaning of a noun or pronoun.

- The **tall, athletic** boy banged his head against a shelf.

  Vs

  The boy banged his head against a shelf.

- The car **with the red roof** is on fire.

  Vs

  The car is on fire.

Mechanics of Writing

Circumstances

These are words or phrases that tell us the **how**, **where**, or **why** regarding events taking place.

They are also known as adverbial phrases and are easily recognisable.

- The baby (subject) + was put (process) + in the bassinet. (circumstance)
- Some students (subject) + struggled (process) + constantly. (circumstance)

The mechanics of writing show how parts of speech function in sentences.

participants = nouns or noun phrases

processes = verbs

attributes = adjectives or adjectival phrases

circumstances = adverbs or adverbial phrases

WORK SHEET 41

Mechanics of Writing

Participants are the nouns that propel the action of the sentence forward.

I Underline the participants and replace them with ones of your own.

1 Many of the pirates followed a strange code of conduct.

2 The furry kitten clawed its way up my leg.

3 My younger sister has bought a giant bag of peanuts.

4 The old church is going to collapse any day now.

5 They dug their way to freedom.

6 Dhruv bought a new shirt from FabIndia yesterday.

7 Right now, the state of the economy is critical.

8 I gave the Red Cross a donation.

9 Oh, put it in the freezer.

10 Nora kicked the ball hard.

Mechanics of Writing

Processes tell us what the participants are or were doing. They move the plot of the sentence forward.

I Identify the processes—mental, material or rational—taking place in the following sentences.

1 All of the puppies had been chewing the furniture.

____

2 Did the players understand the rules of the game?

____

3 The young driver did not know the difference between the brake and the accelerator.

____

4 Shruti is being very attentive in class.

____

5 The miners have to work carefully in the narrow space.

____

6 Pooja painted her bedroom pink.

____

7 I was waiting for the bus.

____

8 Maya has been practising the piano all day.

____

9 Will you come to the library with me?

____

10 What are you mumbling about?

____

11 I will be fourteen next year.

____

12 We had been wondering where to go?

____

Mechanics of Writing

Attributes add meaning to nouns. They elaborate on the qualities of the participants.

I Circle the attributes in the following sentences. Underline the objects to which they refer.

1 We waited at the narrow opening of the cave.

2 The announcer's loud voice makes you want to scream.

3 Cher's costume has more glittering stones than a diamond mine.

4 In the dense jungle, Tarzan lost his way.

5 Those poisonous fish from South America aren't as rare as you'd think.

6 I would love a cup of strong, dark coffee.

7 The tired, hungry workers stopped for lunch.

8 The letter from Kayla was full of good news.

9 I bought a pack of batteries for my dad.

10 The clown in baggy pants tumbled across the circus ring.

Mechanics of Writing

Circumstances tell us how, when, where, why or for how long things happen.

I Circle the circumstances in the following sentences. Rewrite the sentences using different circumstances.

1 There in the distance stood the haunted castle.

____

2 With great force, the rocket cleared the planet's atmosphere.

____

3 Some of the children played quietly in the playground.

____

4 Towards evening, the horses were found by the shed.

____

5 Has she been to the *mela* lately?

____

6 He spoke too fast for the audience to follow clearly.

____

7 I'm going home soon.

____

8 Water dripped constantly from the tap.

____

9 Let's go out for dinner.

____

10 Boil the water for five minutes.

____

11 I'm going swimming in the lake.

____

Quoting, Paraphrasing and Block Quotations

Quoting

Use quotation marks when you have text that is taken word-for-word from the source.

- Bartleby said, "I purchased a fine fat goose for my wife."
- "I often use a rusty fork to comb my woolly beard," Fred replied.

Paraphrasing

If you are summarising someone's statements, then you paraphrase. No quotation marks are needed. Paraphrasing is helpful if there is a lot of information to summarise or if the original text is very vague and paraphrasing can help state it more clearly.

- Justin hinted at his extensive travels by telling me about his favourite cities.
- The constitution was based on the principle that all people are born with the same rights.

Paraphrasing is the process of rewriting the ideas of a passage in your own voice, to enhance the text's clarity and the author's intended meaning. Unlike a summary that reduces a text to only its main points and primary supporting ideas, paraphrasing a passage must present each idea clearly and fully, starting at the beginning of a passage and following sequentially each idea until each has been restated with as much clarity as possible. A person reading a paraphrase must not just feel that he or she has understood the original text, but also has a glimpse of the style of the original.

Guide to Paraphrasing

1. Read the original passage until you understand its full meaning.
2. Mark words or phrases whose meanings are vague or ambiguous. Find synonyms to replace the more complex words in the original text.

Quoting, Paraphrasing and Block Quotations

3. Set the original aside and write your paraphrase on a separate sheet of paper.
4. Edit the sentences to make sure their structure flows smoothly.
5. Check your version with the original to make sure that you have accurately expressed all the relevant information in the new form.
6. Use quotation marks to identify any unique term or phrase you have borrowed exactly from the source.
7. If the original text has examples to clarify its ideas or support its argument, mention it in your paraphrase. You don't have to explain the example, but mention the author's use of them.
8. A paraphrase aims to simplify the portion of the text. In the case of brackets, judge if the information provided clarifies the author's point.
9. Remember to cite the author of the piece you are paraphrasing—the author's name (last name, if the full name has been introduced earlier) and the name of the source (unless introduced earlier).

Read the paraphrase of the play given on page 24.

The scene opens with much consternation as Lady Bracknell interrogates Jack to determine his suitability. Jack ruefully explains that he was found in a handbag abandoned in a railway station.

LESSON 9

Quoting, Paraphrasing and Block Quotations

Lady Bracknell is shocked at what she perceives to be Jack's cavalier attitude regarding his parentage. Jack goes on to explain that a Thomas Cardew found him in Victoria Station and that he has no idea about the identity of his biological parents. Lady Bracknell expresses extreme displeasure, stating unequivocally that one's lineage was a testament of character. Jack's only response is to sheepishly offer to bring in the handbag in question.

Block Quotations

If you have a really long quotation, you use a block quotation. Use block quotations sparingly.

- In block quotations, the entire quote is tabbed.
- A block quotation is preceded by a colon instead of a comma.

⇨ Everybody loved Verne's prized pig collection. Regarding an incident with his neighbour, Verne stated:

> I never understood what Roger was up to until I saw him go into that barn over yonder with several zucchini and a roll of duct tape. I knew he was up to no good. When I seen what he was up to, I called the sheriff. The sheriff came up to the barn and arrested that carpetbagger before he could do much damage.

Verne states that Roger was no longer allowed in the barn. Squealy just hadn't been the same since the incident.

When quoting poetry, try to maintain the pattern or style of the text.

⇨ In her poem, "My life closed twice before its close—", Emily Dickinson writes that: "Parting is all we know of heaven/And all we need of hell" (lines 7-8).

Quoting, Paraphrasing and Block Quotations

I Write a paraphrase of the following passage.

At the end of the Palaeozoic Era (570-245 million years ago), there was a massive extinction where a majority of the life forms on earth—plants, animals, land and sea creatures—were wiped out. A few species survived this extinction and many new life forms made their appearance. One group of new creatures to make an appearance were the dinosaurs.

The first dinosaurs appeared on earth about 230 million years ago, in what is known as the "Triassic Period". The earth was totally different then from what it is today. Apart from the fact that we do not see dinosaurs walking around today, most of the landscape also looked different. Plants and trees, as we know, had not yet appeared on the surface of the earth. There were only some prehistoric plants (like ferns and moss). This was the time when the earth was still recovering from the massive extinction that had happened at the end of the Palaeozoic Era. The earth takes millions of years to recover from this kind of extinction. So when the first dinosaurs appeared on the earth, there were not too many species of animals and plants around. The earth itself was a harsh and inhospitable place to live in.

Quoting, Paraphrasing & Block Quotations

I Write a paraphrase of the following passage.

Compound eyes are found in some groups of animals like crustaceans and insects. These eyes are not made of just one lens like ours, but of thousands of small units. Each of them works like a light detection unit. These units are called ommatidia, which consist of a long tube with a lens on one side and a photoreceptor cell on the other. The final image formed in the brain of the insect is derived from the inputs of all these units, like a mosaic of dark and white spots.

The number of ommatidia an insect has in its eye determines how well it can see. Grasshoppers have fewer ommatidia so they cannot see in great detail. Honeybees and fruit flies are slightly better off, as they have a higher number of these units. The images formed by these eyes are coarse and lack fine details. Also, they cannot see over a great distance. They can see only a few feet in front of them.

Compound eyes are very useful to insects when they are flying. They are better movement detectors than a simple eye.

Summary Writing

Unlike paraphrasing, which is to express someone else's ideas in your own words, a summary aims to distil only the most essential points of someone else's work.

Paraphrase and summary are indispensable tools in essay writing because they allow you to include other people's ideas without cluttering up your essay with too many quotations. You should be guided in your choice of which tool to use by considering how much of the detail from your source is relevant to your argument. If all your reader needs to know is the bare bones, then summarise.

A summary must clearly lay out the main focus of text. In cases where the topic sentence is not immediately clear, use the tone of the text to infer this.

To summarise a longer text, you should follow these steps for each section or chapter of the text; for a shorter piece, you can apply them to the entire text:

1. Find the most important or salient line of the text that explains what the passage or piece is about. This is your topic sentence.
2. Find two or three main ideas and important details that support your topic sentence and show how they are related. Try to address each of them in your summary.
3. Combine several main ideas into a single sentence.
4. Do not include trivial information or unimportant details.
5. Do not repeat information.
6. Try and restrict your summary to a single paragraph unless asked otherwise.
7. The last step in writing a summary is the conclusion. State what you feel was the purpose of the story or article, or what the author accomplished through the writing. Avoid injecting any of your own thoughts. Do not state how you feel the story should have ended or how you might have written it.

When writing a summary, pay close attention to the tone and voice used to describe characters. The essay that follows has a very scientific tone, and so the author uses bold, sweeping statements to get his point across. When summarising a particularly long passage or book, quote phrases or lines from the text to highlight the author's style of writing and emphasise the genre of the piece (horror, romance, clinical, etc.).

Summary Writing

Read the essay given below and the summary given on the next page. Note the economy of words in the summary.

Black Holes

Black Holes are objects in our universe which have such unimaginably high gravity that not even light can escape them.

When you throw a ball upwards, it goes up some distance and returns, because the gravity of the earth pulls the ball back. If you throw the ball harder, it goes higher but eventually does come back. What if you were to throw a ball at a speed of about 11 km per second? Then the ball would escape the gravity of the earth, and go into space. This is what happens to the space shuttle, whose huge engines are required to give it this speed, which is called the escape velocity of the earth. But now imagine an object with such gravitational pull that the escape velocity is larger than 3,00,000 km per second! This awe-inspiring speed is the speed of light. And if light cannot escape from the object, we cannot see it. That is why we call such an object a Black Hole.

Black Holes are not just the stuff of science fiction. Scientists now have fairly robust evidence that such objects do indeed exist in our universe. There might even be one such monster near the centre of the Milky Way galaxy.

How does a Black Hole form? An ordinary star like the sun gives out light and heat because of nuclear reactions taking place inside it. Once the nuclear fuel burns out, the gravity of the star makes it contract, till other forces come into play to stop the contraction. If the mass of the star is larger than about four or five times the mass of the sun (about 3,00,000 earth masses), it could become a Black Hole.

Black Holes are truly strange beasts; the lightest of them is around five times the mass of the sun, and yet it is only a few kilometres across! Nothing which falls into the Black Hole, including light, would ever be able to escape the crushing gravitational force. And such a Black Hole would be a baby Black Hole! Astronomers have found some evidence of a super massive Black Hole near the centre of the Milk Way which is about a million or more times the mass of the sun.

Black Holes were first conjectured by the French mathematician Laplace (1749-1827) in 1796 but it was only after Einstein formulated his theory of relativity that scientists could actually understand their formation.

Summary Writing

And now read the summary.

The author of "Black Holes" attempts to explain the astronomical phenomenon of Black Holes through a simple metaphor of a ball being thrown up, designed to explain the escape velocity of the earth. Black Holes were originally theorised by the mathematician Laplace in 1796 but could not be understood until Einstein proposed his theory of relativity. Black Holes are the result of large burnt out stars, "four or five times the mass of the sun", contracting under their own gravity and creating a "hole" in space from which nothing, not even light, can escape.

Summary Writing

I Read the following passage and write a summary.

Imagine living in a world where you cannot feel the difference between rough and smooth objects. Simple acts like running one's fingers through sand on a beach or feeling a smooth satin scarf would become utterly meaningless and frustrating. Thankfully, most of us have normal functional hands whose powers we take for granted in our everyday life. We are able to experience a thousand different things by touching them. How does touching an object with one's hand evoke these sensations which vary in myriad subtle ways? How do we "feel" the difference between corduroy and polyester? The answer lies in the skin that encases our body, especially the skin on our palms, which has exquisite powers of detection and discrimination. For instance, one can tell if a mango is ripe or raw by holding it gently and applying pressure on it. We check the air pressure in our bicycle tyres and decide whether we need to refill or not by just pressing them with our fingers.

We can also figure out shapes without looking at them. One can distinguish an orange from a banana with one's eyes closed. The skin on our fingers acts as a sensor that can differentiate smoothness, roughness, stickiness, softness, hardness, heat, cold, vibration, motion and much more. It can also differentiate between patterns. For instance, we can tell most of the letters of the alphabet embossed in nameplates by feeling them with our fingers. The visually impaired can read quite efficiently with their fingertips. In the Braille method, each letter is represented by a different pattern of embossed dots that visually impaired persons can differentiate with their fingertips.

Essay Writing 1

Essays can be written in a number of different styles, depending on the subject and the purpose.

- A **descriptive essay** describes a process or the characteristics or structure of something.
- A **narrative essay** usually narrates a sequence of events. It may give background information, or the consequences of actions.
- A **persuasive essay** tries to convince the reader about something through a series of arguments and may make recommendations. It presents an idea or point of view. By implication, it tries to persuade another person to change or at least consider changing their opinion about the subject.

Narrative essays frequently contain all the necessary components of action development: protagonist, setting, goal, obstacle, climax and resolution. When writing in the narrative style, it is important to pay close attention to order, chronology and mood. Many descriptive elements should be included.

Tone and Voice

Tone and voice are the elements that tell us about the circumstances surrounding a statement or scenario. They can be as simple as punctuation or as complex as elements within the parts of speech.

➔ Run.

This is a simple statement.

➔ Run!

The statement now takes on an urgent tone.

➔ Run?

The statement is questioning.

➔ She ran frantically.

The use of an adverb introduces an element of action or danger.

➔ She broke into a quick jog.

The statement describes a calm state of events.

The tone is the feel of the piece, the mood and the emotion it evokes. This is created by many things, including word choice, sentence structure and unity of images and metaphors. Depending on the choices a writer makes, he or she can create an ominous tone, a comical tone, a sarcastic tone, or anything in between.

Essay Writing 1

➔ Grey snow fell like ash from the sky and the smoky black clouds above seemed to pour from an invisible fire. When the flakes settled, they covered everything like a sheet over a corpse.

In the above sentences, something simple is being described, but because of the word choices and the imagery, the tone is very ominous. One senses that something bad is about to happen.

➔ The snow that fell from the sky was as white and puffy as whipped cream over hot chocolate. The dark clouds reminded me of chocolate muffins and the spinning flakes as they settled on the ground might have been glazed gems of sugar.

Here the same scene is described, but it's happier as if viewed by a character inside a cosy home. Instead of a story about storms and death, this might be better suited to a scene about a family holiday.

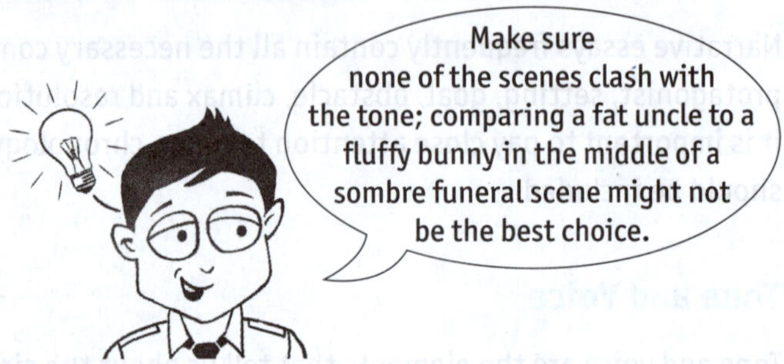

Try to use images, words and sentence structures that suit the mood of your story. Choose a tone that is appropriate for the type of piece you are writing and the emotions you are trying to evoke.

LESSON 11

Essay Writing 1

The voice is the attitude of the narrator or author and the speech patterns and inflections that reveal his attitude and purpose. This is indicated by the way a text is 'spoken' and the attitude it reveals and this can also have an effect on tone.

A first-person narrator might relay the same information in several different ways:

- As I entered the restaurant, I inadvertently collided with another gentleman—and of course begged his pardon—but he ignored me and continued about his business. I thought that was rude of him.

The narrator is describing the scene politely and professionally. One gathers that the narrator is calm, civil and urbane. Compare it with this writer:

- I was going into the restaurant when this twit bumped into me. I muttered an apology, but he didn't even listen to me. He just kind of shoved aside and went back to all his important business. Who did he think he was? Twit!

The voice of this piece is less formal, but more colourful. Hints of sarcasm and irritation are noticeable.

Here are a few other essay topics you could explore:

- What is more important: actions or intentions?
- Why is telling the truth important?
- Do you believe children should have a curfew?
- Do you think you are a good role model, and why?

Essay Writing 1

I Read the following passage. It is the introductory passage of a short story.

The falling rays of the sun cast a golden mist in the evening sky at Giza. As the last flock of tourists gathered to watch a sound-and-light show retired from the comforts of cushioned seating to a humpback ride back to the hotel, the daylong crowded narrow lanes now became a private walkway for young Naseer, heading back home from his evening Quran classes. Naseer glanced back the headlines of *Al Khuit*, the local evening newspaper. His eyes followed the faint light from flickering lanterns along the road to read:
"Dry winds on the rise; Khamsin may hit Giza."

The Khamsin—the violent dust storms that rise from the hot Sahara desert fill the air with waves of sand and cast a murky cloud, blanketing the sunlight. Naseer had read that once when the French army, under the command of General Napoleon Bonaparte, decided to invade Egypt, the deadly Khamsin arose from the east of Giza. The natives went to take cover, while the French did not react until it was too late, then choked and fainted in the blinding, suffocating walls of dust. Anything caught in the Khamsin gets its soul sucked out of the body.

Let's break down the paragraph above into its stylistic components.

- Protagonist: Naseer is introduced at the very beginning of the story.
- Setting: Giza and the Khamsin are the setting. We learn about the time of day (dusk), the history of the region and the legend of the Khamsin.
- Goal: The goal is not made clear (yet), but we know it involves the coming storm.
- Obstacle: Possibly the Khamsin.
- Climax: Possibly Naseer's attempts at surviving the storm.
- Resolution: Not clear yet.

Essay Writing 1

1 Finish the story. How do you think it will it end?

2 The author has quite a fondness for metaphors. Can you identify them?

Essay Writing 1

3 How would you rewrite this story in a positive manner? Pay attention to the tone used.

Essay Writing 1

I Read the following essay by a thirteen-year-old student.

I feel that we should have a law that tells us not to leave trash in parks or beaches. If there is a law already in place, then I suggest we take strong measures to enforce it.

I think this because a lot of people that leave trash destroy the natural beauty of such places. When this happens a lot of animals die. Some become or are close to becoming extinct.

Here are some reasons why we should have or enforce this law. Lots of people don't pick up trash, mostly plastic bags. Turtles eat jellyfish, as you may know, but what I'm getting at is that plastic bags look like jellyfish in a turtle's eyes. Then when the turtle swallows the bag, it chokes because the bag is so thick. The turtle then dies. Some birds get their beaks stuck in plastic bottles and then they die from starvation.

Here is an example of how we can clean our beaches. I remember every summer we would have a picnic lunch. With four people in my family we can sometimes create a lot of trash. My mom always brings a "trash bag" and when we are done eating we have to put every scrap of trash in the bag. We even clean up the ground in our immediate area and put other people's trash in our bag. We try to live by the creed: "Leave a place better than you find it." At the end of our day, we take the trash bag out to the parking lot and place it in a trash can.

Some people might think that they should not have to clean up. Perhaps they think that is somebody else's job. But nobody wants to go to a stinky, messy, polluted area . . . and the animals that live there do not want to have a messy home. If it is too costly to have people patrol these places and fine those who leave their trash behind, then maybe it's time to consider not allowing people to bring food or beverages to parks or beaches. I would be sad to see that happen, though, because I enjoy a picnic lunch on the beach.

1 What is the central theme of this essay?

Essay Writing 1

2 What solutions does the author offer?

3 How does the author frame her argument? Does the author use real life examples or hypothetical scenarios?

4 Do you agree with the author's thesis? Do you agree with her solution? How would you frame this argument?

WORK SHEET 50

Essay Writing 1

I **Why is fast food unhealthy? Write down at least one idea for both sides of the argument. Be clear on the action you wish the reader to take. Make sure you have at least three facts to support your opinion.**

Essay Writing 2

Writing an essay will often call for research. First, determine what research you need to do:

1. Make a list of what you already know about your topic.
2. Decide what other information you are most likely to need.
3. Make a note of how you plan to get this information. Will you visit a library? Search the internet? Interview someone?
4. Structuring—underline/highlight relevant points. Make a checklist.

Drafting

Sketch out a rough plan for organising your writing.

- Working thesis

  Increased motorcycle use demands traffic reorganisation (more motorcycles means more traffic jams).
- Introduction
  - Give the background and overview of the situation (motorcycle sales are up)
  - State the purpose (to offer solutions to the problem)
- Body
  - Describe the current situation (research on traffic incidents)
  - Describe the problem in detail (statistics, cars vs. motorcycles)
  - Present possible solutions (pedestrian walkway, separate lane)
- Conclusion
  - Discuss possible cost and space limitation of solutions
  - Summarise the benefits of the solutions

LESSON 12

Essay Writing 2

Writing process

- Try to keep all the information close at hand and arranged in the order of your plan.
- Try to work in stretches of at least fifteen minutes; writing will get easier as you go along.
- Don't get bogged down with details such as word choice or mechanics.
- A draft is always rough; concentrate on just getting your ideas down.

Revising

After you have finished a draft, take a fresh look at it to make sure it is complete, clear and effective. Revising is very important.

- Do you have a good title? Does it tell the reader what the essay is about?
- Is your main argument clearly stated, and does it contain a topic and a comment?
- Does the introduction catch the reader's attention?
- How does the essay indicate your stance on the topic?
- Are the points clearly linked by logical transitions?
- How does it conclude?
- Read your draft aloud to make sure it flows smoothly and to find typos and other mistakes.
- Proofread it one last time.

Some possible topics for essays can be:

- Global warming: Causes and effects
- How has the rise of twenty-four-hour news channels changed our view on information?
- Do sports stars or celebrities bear any responsibility for be[illegible]ole models for children?
- Are exams a proper method of evaluating students?

Book Review

A book review is a description, analysis and evaluation on the quality, meaning and significance of a book. It is not simply a retelling. It focuses on the book's purpose, content and style. A book review is a reaction to the text in which strengths and weaknesses of the material are examined. It states what the author has tried to do, evaluates how well (in the opinion of the reviewer) the author succeeds, and presents evidence to support this statement.

Writing the review:

1. State the author's purpose in writing the book. Sometimes authors state their purpose in the preface or the first chapter. When they do not, you may infer the book's purpose by trying to answer these questions:
   a. Why did the author write on this subject as opposed to any other?
   b. What is the point of view of the text?
   c. What does the text attempt to do? Does it tell a story, introduce a new concept, or examine an existing concept or phenomenon?
   d. What genre does the book fall under? Knowledge of the genre means a glancing familiarity with other works in that area.
   e. Who is the intended audience?
2. Explain the way the author fulfils his purpose or illustrates his theme. Illustrate your remarks with specific references and quotations.
   a. **Description:** The author presents scenarios and events by giving specific details that appeal to the reader's imagination. Description presents background and setting. Its primary purpose is to help the reader realise, through as many details as possible, the way things (and people) are, within the universe of the book.
   b. **Narration:** The author narrates the story of a series of events, usually presented in chronological order. In a novel, however, chronological order may be violated for the sake of the plot. The emphasis in narration, in both fiction and non-fiction, is on the events. Narration tells what has happened.
   c. **Exposition:** The author uses explanation and analysis to present a subject or to clarify an idea. Exposition presents the facts about a subject or an issue as clearly as possible.

Book Review

d. **Argument:** The author attempts to establish the truth of a statement or to convince the reader of its falsity. The purpose is to persuade the reader to believe something and perhaps to act on that belief. Argument takes sides on an issue.

e. What is the author's style? Is it formal or informal? Evaluate the quality of the writing style on the basis of coherence, clarity, originality, correct use of language, conciseness, character development and fluidity.

f. Scan the table of contents. It can help understand how the book is organised and will aid in determining the author's main ideas and how they are developed.

g. How does the author use descriptive, narrative and persuasive styles in the book.

h. How did the book affect you? Were any previous ideas you had on the subject changed, abandoned, or reinforced due to this book?

i. How well has the book achieved its goal?

j. Would you recommend this book to others? Why?

3. If relevant, make note of the book's format—layout, binding, typography, etc. Are there maps or illustrations? Do they aid understanding or add to the appeal of the book?

4. Summarise (briefly), analyse and comment on the book's content. You can include a final assessment or simply restate your thesis. Do not introduce any new ideas at this point.

When Reviewing Fiction

Remember to comment on the following:

<u>Characters</u>

1. How well developed are the characters?
2. What is the author's attitude towards the characters?
3. Does further character development or growth occur?
4. Is there a range of characters (gender, race, etc...)?
5. Is there any character you liked or disliked?

Book Review

Theme

1. What is/are the major theme(s)?
2. How are they revealed and developed?

Plot

1. How are the various elements of plot (introduction, suspense, climax, conclusion) handled?
2. What is the relationship of plot to character development?
3. What are the elements of mystery and suspense?
5. How is conflict, if any, resolved?
6. Are there sub-plots and how are they related to the main plot?

Style

1. What are the qualities of the writing (e.g., simplicity, clarity)?
2. What are the "emotional qualities" of the writing (e.g., humour, wit, satire)?
3. What are the "aesthetic qualities" of the writing (e.g., pace, flow)?
4. What stylistic devices are employed (e.g., metaphors, clichés, similes, oxymorons, hyperbole)?
5. How effective is the dialogue?

Setting

1. What is the setting and how significant a role does it play?
2. Is a sense of atmosphere evoked, and how?

When Reviewing Biographies

1. Does the book give a holistic picture of the subject?
2. What phases of the subject's life receive the greatest treatment and is this treatment justified?
3. What is the point of view of the author?
4. How is the subject matter organised—chronologically, retrospectively, etc.?

Book Review

5. What source materials were used in the preparation of the biography?
6. What important new facts about the subject's life are revealed in the book?
7. How does the biography compare with others about the same person?

When Reviewing History and Other Non-fiction

1. With what subject or period does the book deal?
2. Is the account given in broad outline or in detail?
3. What is the point of view or thesis of the author?

When Reviewing Poetry

1. Is this a work of originality and individuality?
2. What kind of poem (epic, lyrical, elegiac, etc.) is it?
3. What poetical devices have been used (rhyme, rhythm, figures of speech, imagery, etc.) and to what effect?
4. What is the central concern of the poem and is it effectively expressed?

Book Review

I Write a book review on any book that you've read this year.

WORK SHEET 51

Book Review

LESSON 14

Movie Review

The process involved in writing a movie review is similar to that used for writing a book review.

The length of the review can be as short as a single paragraph or as long as a few pages.

Parts of a Review

1. Title

   The title is usually the name of the movie.

2. Theme statement

   The theme statement tells us what the movie is about. You should also mention what genre it is—comedy, action, adventure, documentary, drama, fantasy or horror.

3. Plot summary

   The summary describes what happens in the movie. It should describe the setting, characters, time period and style of the movie.

4. Critique

   This is where you give your opinion of the film, with specific details from the movie to support your opinion. A good reviewer can also highlight what could have been done to improve the film.

   Some things to keep in mind while composing your critique should be:

   Did you like the movie? Why?

   Do you feel the movie was successful as a representation of its genre?

   Were you impressed by the direction, acting, writing, special effects or any other aspect of the movie?

Movie Review

Would you recommend this movie to others?

Did you learn something from this movie? Or was its main purpose to entertain?

Read the following review for ***The Fantastic Mr Fox***.

The Fantastic Mr Fox is an animated action-adventure movie based on the book by Roald Dahl. The movie is a modern twist on the book, which is about a fox who has to outwit three mean farmers to feed his family and friends.

The movie and the book are similar in plot but director Wes Anderson has George Clooney, the voice of Mr Fox, play the character as a retired fox bank-robber instead of a typical creature of the woods. The movie opens with Mr Fox at content in his suburban home, wistfully imagining his youth as a crook, stealing chickens and apple cider from three local farmers. The movie also includes a new character Kristofferson, the nephew of Mr Fox who is staying with the family and is every bit the dashing adventurer Mr Fox is. Mr Fox's own son Ash, is shy and awkward, trying desperately to be cool and popular like his dad. Part of the drama of the movie is the jealously between Ash and Kristofferson as they vie for Mr Fox's attention. The rest of the movie is fraught with tension as Mr Fox attempts to provide for his family and keep them and his community safe from the farmers.

The Fantastic Mr Fox is playful, humorous movie that is at its core heart warming. It is action packed, with a fantastic cast of famous voice actors who breathe life into what could have otherwise been two-dimensional characters. The market is rife with remakes of beloved children's books but none have been as charming, magical or fresh as this adaptation by Wes Anderson. The book's core message—our differences make us special—is faithfully maintained despite the sometimes-jarring animation.

Movie Review

I **Write a reveiw for a movie you saw this year. What did you think of it? What was it about?**

Movie Review

Movie Review

I **Write a reveiw for a movie you disliked. What didn't you like about it? How could it have been better?**

LESSON 15

E-mail Writing

The ubiquitous and casual nature of e-mail makes it the preferred method of communication for many people nowadays. E-mail is quickly supplanting letters as the primary means of written communication.

E-mails fall somewhere between a letter and a phone call in terms of communication. Its near-instantaneous nature frees it from the rigidity of a letter, but it also allows its writer time to coolly collect and formulate a response that a phone call cannot. E-mails and letters are stylistically similar but vary in subtle ways.

Parts of an e-mail:

Address: This is the e-mail address and often the name of the person to whom you are writing an e-mail.

Subject: The subject of an e-mail is the equivalent of a summary statement for your message. Always include a meaningful subject line; this helps clarify what your message is about and may also help the recipient prioritise reading your e-mail.

Salutation: This is a fancy word for greeting. The most common salutation in an e-mail is "Dear ..."

Body: This is the main part of the e-mail where you write what you have to say to the person. Unlike letters, e-mails are meant for quick, simple communication. Due to the limitations of formatting and layout, anything longer than a few paragraphs is probably best sent as a separate attachment. Most people have a limited attention span with e-mail—if they receive a lot of mail, you want to get to the main message in the shortest possible space.

Closing: The closing is the ending to your message. There are many closing remarks to choose from depending on your relationship with the recipient. Some popular ones are: Sincerely, Love, Best wishes, etc.

Signature: This identifies the writer of the message. It appears directly under the closing. If you are sure the person will know who you are, just sign your first name. If not, add your last name.

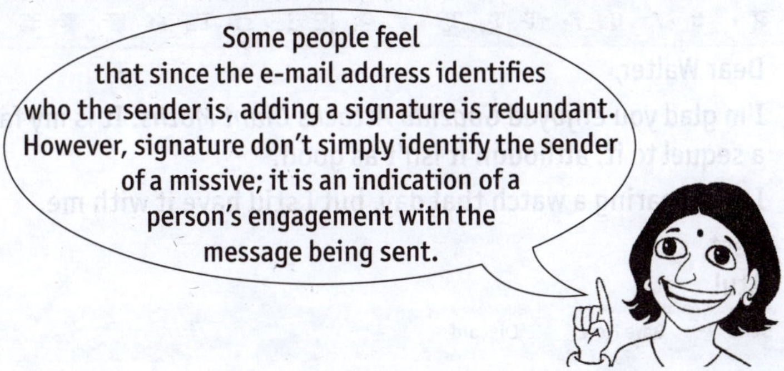

E-mail Writing

Send | Save Now | Discard

To: Atul Ramalingam [atuldagr8@gvschool.co.in]

Add Cc | Add Bcc

Subject: Wednesday Movie

Attach a file

« Plain Text | Check Spelling ▾

Dear Atul,

It was great seeing you this Wednesday. You were right, that movie was hilarious. I'll return the CD when I see you again.

I just wanted to check—are you missing a watch? Mom found a black digital watch in the living room yesterday. It doesn't belong to anyone here, but I don't remember if you were wearing a watch or not when you came to visit.

Let me know if it is yours and I'll bring it to school.

Cheers,
Walter

Send | Save Now | Discard

Send | Save Now | Discard

To: Walter Snoodgrass [GotuBath@bathe.com]

Add Cc | Add Bcc

Subject: Re: Wednesday Movie

Attach a file

« Plain Text | Check Spelling ▾

Dear Walter,

I'm glad you enjoyed *Godzilla Attacks Giant Moths*. It is my favourite monster movie. There's even a sequel to it, although it isn't as good.

I was wearing a watch that day, but I still have it with me.

Best,
Atul

Send | Save Now | Discard

WORK SHEET 54

E-mail Writing

I **You and your friend are planning to throw a surprise party later this week. Compose an e-mail to your friend discussing the logistics of the party—venue, food, music and games.**

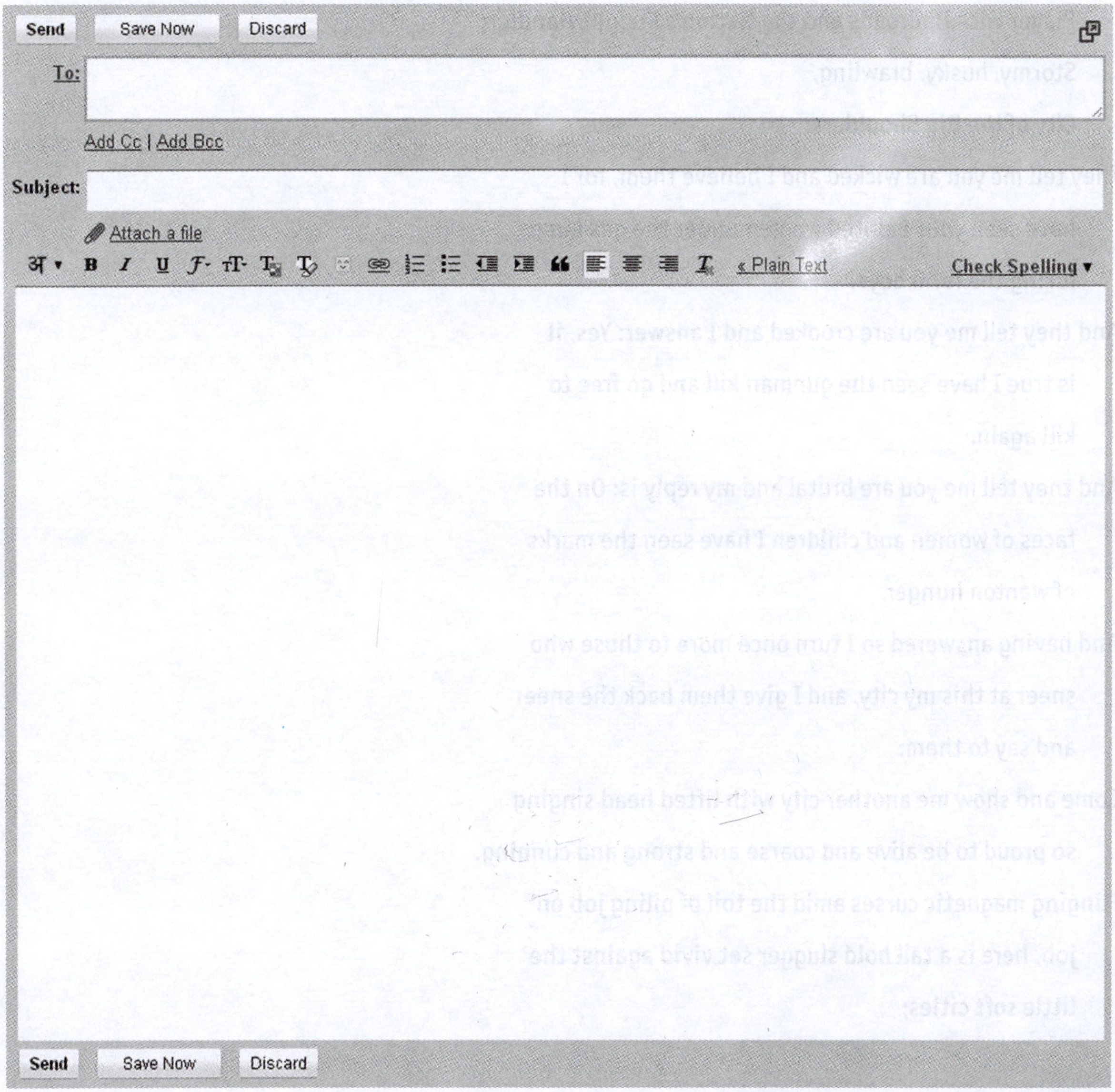

Revision 2

I **Read the following poem by Charles Sandburg and answer the questions that follow.**

Chicago

HOG Butcher for the World,
Tool Maker, Stacker of Wheat,
Player with Railroads and the Nation's Freight Handler;
Stormy, husky, brawling,
City of the Big Shoulders:
They tell me you are wicked and I believe them, for I
have seen your painted women under the gas lamps
luring the farm boys.
And they tell me you are crooked and I answer: Yes, it
is true I have seen the gunman kill and go free to
kill again.
And they tell me you are brutal and my reply is: On the
faces of women and children I have seen the marks
of wanton hunger.
And having answered so I turn once more to those who
sneer at this my city, and I give them back the sneer
and say to them:
Come and show me another city with lifted head singing
so proud to be alive and coarse and strong and cunning.
Flinging magnetic curses amid the toil of piling job on
job, here is a tall bold slugger set vivid against the
little soft cities;

Revision 2

Fierce as a dog with tongue lapping for action, cunning
as a savage pitted against the wilderness,
Bareheaded,
Shoveling,
Wrecking,
Planning,
Building, breaking, rebuilding,
Under the smoke, dust all over his mouth, laughing with
white teeth,
Under the terrible burden of destiny laughing as a young
man laughs,
Laughing even as an ignorant fighter laughs who has
never lost a battle,
Bragging and laughing that under his wrist is the pulse.
and under his ribs the heart of the people,
Laughing!
Laughing the stormy, husky, brawling laughter of
Youth, half-naked, sweating, proud to be Hog
Butcher, Tool Maker, Stacker of Wheat, Player with
Railroads and Freight Handler to the Nation.

1 What words in the poem illustrate the personification of the city?

2 According to the poet, what are the problems with the city of Chicago? Give reasons to support your answer.

3 This is a very visual poem. Identify the imagery used (metaphors, similes, allusions, etc.).

Revision 2

4 **Write a poem about your city.**

Revision 2

II **Read the following poem and answer the questions that follow.**

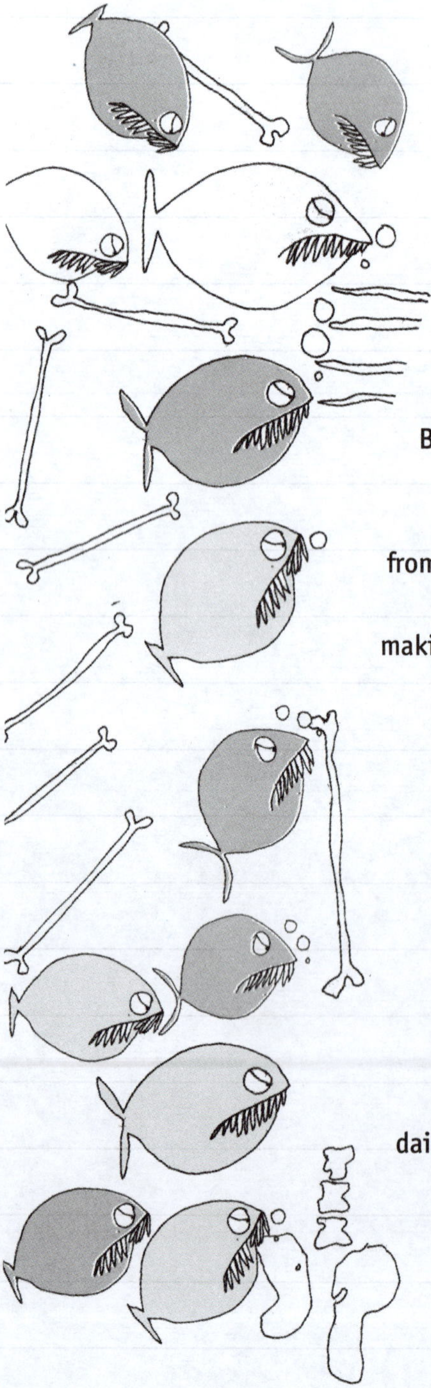

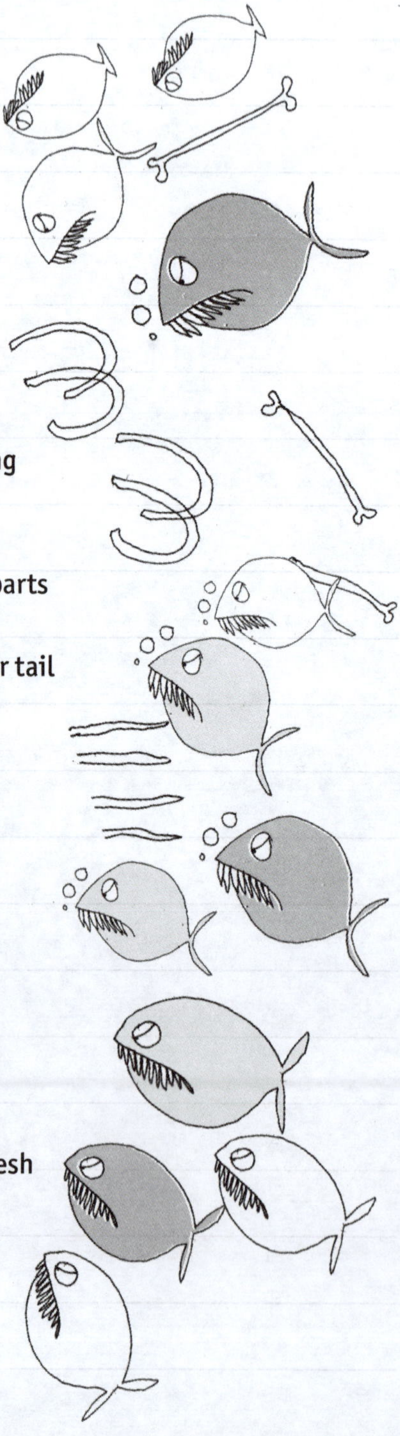

Piranhas

Picked
to the quick
Stripped
of everything
Barecoldandshivering
Dissected
subtracted
from the sum of all its parts
Bones sticking out
making neither head nor tail
sharpetched
against the light
A hieroglyph
of slant and curve
of straight
and slightly bent
Twisted remnant
of the feast
a fish rippedtorn
by delicate fingers
those piranhas
daily demolishers of flesh
stained
until licked
and
polished
clean

Revision 2

1 What is this poem about?

2 What effect do the removed spaces (Barecoldandshivering) have? How do you read it?

3 How are the piranhas described? What is the tone of the piece?

4 The poet has invented a word by combining two others—sharpetched. What do you think it means? (Hint: Use the context of the poem to figure it out.) What words have been combined together? What words can you make up?

Revision 2

III Read the following extract and answer the questions that follow.

The Rescue Mission

The Malwa king's army and equipage were magnificent. Clearly, Devgupta was a very wealthy king, ruling over a highly prosperous kingdom. What else could account for the riches—elephants in thousands with glorious canopies, pure-bred horses with jewelled plumes, ornaments of beauteous craftsmanship and colour, pearl necklaces reflecting the beauty of the heavens in their shimmering beads, jewel-encrusted thrones and conches, and cavernous treasure chests laden with innumerable ornaments and jewels?

Accompanying these were, of course, all the adherents of the Malwa king with heavy iron chains clinking on their feet. Harsha inspected the lot carefully, appointing overseers to take charge of the booty.

Madhava, meanwhile, could barely restrain his impatience. Surely Bhandi could have taken care of all of this! Why was the king wasting precious moments while his sister languished in that fearsome forest? He watched, fretting and fidgeting, as Harsha gave instructions and the insufferable Bhandi strutted about with a smug air.

It was evening before they set out on horseback in search of Rajyasri—just the king, Madhava and a few soldiers who were familiar with the area. The terrain changed in imperceptible ways, from the lush green environs near the camp to the more rugged territory of the hills. A cool breeze blew, signalling the fact that winter was not too far away. They rode through that night and all of the next day, stopping only to eat and water the horses.

By daybreak of the third day, the group managed to reach the outskirts of the Vindhya forest. Huge trees reared in all directions, encircling the jungle, and a shroud of silence seemed to cover it all.

Dismounting, they plunged resolutely into the woods, leading their horses along lines of massive banyan trees, each of whose roots were as thick as a wrestler's arm. The ground beneath their feet was black and hard as iron, and the horses' hooves clanged in a monotonous rhythm as they advanced. An impenetrable roof of thick, leafy branches formed a silent cover, blocking out the sun and making it seem as dark as night within the forest.

Harsha walked on and on, seemingly tireless, while the others stumbled on in his path, the whinnying of horses breaking the heavy stillness, now and again. Bamboos gave way to other kinds of trees—slender, twisting vines, and trees laden with fruits and blossoms. Invisible birds kept up an intermittent twittering, but occasionally, the harsh cry of a vulture could be heard overhead. Madhava found himself wondering how Rajyasri was managing in this brooding, inhospitable place—if she was still alive, that is.

Revision 2

At long last, they came upon a hunter who carried a quiver of bearskin and a thick rope, from which dangled a dead partridge and a hare. The latter's soft, white fur was stained with its blood. Not knowing who Harsha was, the dark, young man nevertheless bowed before him, sensing that he was in the presence of an exalted personage. Wordlessly, he held out the dead creatures to Harsha, but the latter, politely declining the gift, asked, "As you obviously know this region well, have you seen a noble lady and her attendants in this forest at any time in these past few days?"

The hunter shook his head. "I cannot help you, noble sir," he said regretfully, "but I know someone who can. Not far from here, in a thicket of trees at the foot of the mountain, besides the stream, dwells a famous Buddhist ascetic called Divakaramitra, along with his disciples. You could ask him the same question. Perhaps he or his followers have noticed something."

Harsha stiffened at the sound of the mendicant's name and a hopeful look spread over his face. "What a coincidence!" he told Madhava under his breath. "Grahavarman had a young ascetic friend by the same name. I remember him telling father so. Is he the same person then?"

Madhava shrugged his shoulders, but was similarly excited. They thanked the hunter for his help and set off in the direction he had indicated.

Revision 2

1 **What tells us about the Malwa king's wealth?**

2 **What phrases or descriptions create tension in this extract? What is your reaction to the abrupt introduction to Harsha?**

3 **Write a short summary of this passage.**

4 **Imagine you are one of the soldiers on this dangerous mission. You might never see your loved ones again. Write a letter to your family.**

IV Read the following poem and answer the questions that follow.

A Kind of Love Song

You are a prickle on my skin today.
A leaf on my tongue.

You are a pair of swinging legs
from the edge of a table today.

You are a desire to run.

You are an unstoppable giggle today.
A kite unattached to a string.

You are a pair of eyes chasing eyes
in the playfield today.

You are a little blue thing.

You are a secret chamber in my heart today.
An open-window –word.

You are a pair of hands
holding the light for me today.

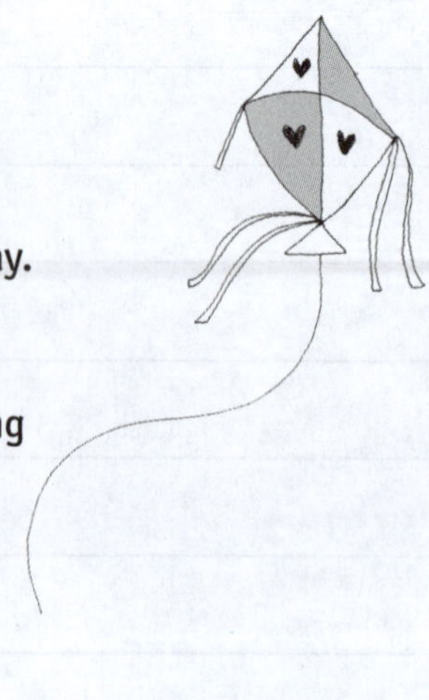

You are a whisper overheard.

You are a strangeness of summer today.
A sudden tingling of rain.

Warm as my breath, you are everything
but yourself today.

How long will you remain?

Revision 2

1 Identify the imagery used (metaphors, similes, allusions, etc.).

2 What is this poem about? What is the tone like? Is it cheerful, hopeful, sad or bleak?

3 "You are a pair of eyes chasing eyes/in the playfield today." What do you think the author means here?

4 What stylistic changes do you observe between "A Kind of Love Song" and "Piranhas"? Use instances from the poems to support your answer.

WORD BANKS Verb Tense

Tenses allow speakers and writers to express exactly what they want to say.

Present Tense Verbs

Tense	Number	1st Person	2nd Person	3rd Person
Simple present	Singular	I **eat** fish.	You **eat** fish.	He/she/it **eats** fish.
	Plural	We **eat** fish.	You **eat** fish.	They **eat** fish.
Present continuous	Singular	I **am eating** fish.	You **are eating** fish.	He/she/it **is eating** fish.
	Plural	We **are eating** fish.	You **are eating** fish.	They **are eating** fish.
Present perfect	Singular	I **have eaten** fish.	You **have eaten** fish.	He/she/it **has eaten** fish.
	Plural	We **have eaten** fish.	You **have eaten** fish.	They **have eaten** fish.
Perfect continuous	Singular	I **have been eating** fish.	You **have been eating** fish.	He/she/it **has been eating** fish.
	Plural	We **have been eating** fish.	You **have been eating** fish.	They **have been eating** fish.

Past Tense Verbs

Tense	Number	1st Person	2nd Person	3rd Person
Simple past	Singular	I **ate** fish.	You **ate** fish.	He/she/it **ate** fish.
	Plural	We **ate** fish.	You **ate** fish.	They **ate** fish.
Past continuous	Singular	I **was eating** fish.	You **were eating** fish.	He/she/it **was eating** fish.
	Plural	We **were eating** fish.	You **were eating** fish.	They **were eating** fish.
Past perfect	Singular	I **had eaten** fish.	You **had eaten** fish.	He/she/it **had eaten** fish.
	Plural	We **had eaten** fish.	You **had eaten** fish.	They **had eaten** fish.
Perfect continuous	Singular	I **had been eating** fish.	You **had been eating** fish.	He/she/it **had been eating** fish.
	Plural	We **had been eating** fish.	You **had been eating** fish.	They **had been eating** fish.

Future Tense Verbs

Tense	Number	1st Person	2nd Person	3rd Person
Simple future	Singular	I **will eat** fish.	You **will eat** fish.	He/she/it **will eat** fish.
	Plural	We **will eat** fish.	You **will eat** fish.	They **will eat** fish.

Future continuous	Singular	I **will be eating** fish.	You **will be eating** fish.	He/she/it **will be eating** fish.
	Plural	We **will be eating** fish.	You **will be eating** fish.	They **will be eating** fish.
Future perfect	Singular	I **will have eaten** fish.	You **will have eaten** fish.	He/she/it **will have eaten** fish.
	Plural	We **will have eaten** fish.	You **will have eaten** fish.	They **will have eaten** fish.
Future Perfect continuous	Singular	I **will have been eating** fish.	You **will have been eating** fish.	He/she/it **will have been eating** fish.
	Plural	We **will have been eating** fish.	You **will have been eating** fish.	They **will have been eating** fish.

We can even add other verbs to clarify our meaning.

- I ***could*** have been eating fish.
- They ***should*** be eating fish.
- He ***might*** have eaten fish.
- We ***can*** eat fish.

Verbs

Auxiliary verbs are helping verbs. They provide extra information about a sentence, which is not given by the main verb.

List of helping (**auxiliary**) verbs

- am, aren't (only in inversion, as in aren't I special?), 'm (as in I'm)
- are, aren't, 're (as in you're)
- be
- been
- can, can't
- could, couldn't
- did, didn't
- do, don't
- does, doesn't
- had, hadn't, 'd (She'd gone out.)
- has, hasn't, 's (She's gone out.)
- have, haven't, 've (I've)
- is, isn't, 's (She's back.)
- may, mayn't
- might, mightn't
- must, mustn't
- ought, oughtn't
- shall, shan't
- should, shouldn't
- was, wasn't
- were, weren't
- will, won't, 'll (she'll)
- would, wouldn't, 'd (I'd go out.)

Irregular Verbs

One of the more frustrating things about tenses is learning the irregular verbs by heart. As you know, the past tense forms of regular verbs end in **ed** or **d**, however irregular verbs just need to be learnt.

Infinitive	Past simple	Past participle
be	was/were	been
beat	beat	beaten
become	became	become
begin	began	begun
bend	bent	bent
bet	bet	bet
bite	bit	bitten
blow	blew	blown
break	broke	broken
bring	brought	brought
build	built	built
burst	burst	burst
buy	bought	bought
catch	caught	caught
choose	chose	chosen
come	came	come
cost	cost	cost
cut	cut	cut
deal	dealt	dealt
dig	dug	dug
do	did	done
draw	drew	drawn
drink	drank	drunk
drive	drove	driven
eat	ate	eaten
fall	fell	fallen

Infinitive	Past simple	Past participle
feed	fed	fed
feel	felt	felt
fight	fought	fought
find	found	found
fly	flew	flown
forbid	forbade	forbidden
forget	forgot	forgotten
freeze	froze	frozen
get	got	got
give	gave	given
go	went	gone
grow	grew	grown
hang	hung	hung
have	had	had
hear	heard	heard
hide	hid	hidden
hit	hit	hit
hold	held	held
hurt	hurt	hurt
keep	kept	kept
know	knew	known
lay	laid	laid
lead	led	led
leave	left	left
lend	lent	lent
let	let	let

WORD BANKS Verb Tense

Infinitive	Past simple	Past participle
lie	lay	lain
light	lit	lit
lose	lost	lost
make	made	made
mean	meant	meant
meet	met	met
pay	paid	paid
put	put	put
read	read	read
ride	rode	ridden
ring	rang	rung
rise	rose	risen
run	ran	run
say	said	said
see	saw	seen
seek	sought	sought
sell	sold	sold
send	sent	sent
set	set	set
sew	sewed	sewn/sewed
shake	shook	shaken
shine	shone	shone
shoot	shot	shot
show	showed	shown
shrink	shrank	shrunk
shut	shut	shut
sing	sang	sung
sink	sank	sunk

Infinitive	Past simple	Past participle
sit	sat	sat
sleep	slept	slept
speak	spoke	spoken
spend	spent	spent
split	split	split
spread	spread	spread
spring	sprang	sprung
stand	stood	stood
steal	stole	stolen
stick	stuck	stuck
sting	stung	stung
stink	stank	stunk
strike	struck	struck
swear	swore	sworn
sweep	swept	swept
swim	swam	swum
swing	swung	swung
take	took	taken
teach	taught	taught
tear	tore	torn
tell	told	told
think	thought	thought
throw	threw	thrown
understand	understood	understood
wake	woke	woken
wear	wore	worn
win	won	won
write	wrote	written

WORD BANKS Pronoun

A pronoun is a substitute for a noun. Some pronouns are: **I, me, she, he, her, him, it, you, they,** and **them.**

Pronouns	Pronoun as subject	Pronoun as object	Pronoun as possessive adjective	Possessive pronoun	Reflexive pronoun
1st Person Singular	I	me	my	mine	myself
2nd Person Singular	you	you	your	yours	yourself
3rd Person Singular	he she it	him her it	his her it	his hers its	himself herself itself
1st Person Plural	we	us	our	ours	ourselves
2nd Person Plural	you	you	your	yours	yourselves
3rd Person Plural	they	them	their	theirs	themselves

WORD BANKS Pronoun

Pronouns Vocabulary Word List

A	**I**	**O**	**U**
all	I	one	us
another	it	other	**W**
any	its	others	we
anybody	itself	our	what
anyone	**M**	ours	whatever
anything	many	ourselves	which
B	me	**S**	whichever
both	mine	several	who
E	more	she	whoever
each	most	some	whom
either	much	somebody	whomever
everybody	my	someone	whose
everyone	myself	something	**Y**
everything	**N**	**T**	you
F	neither	that	your
few	no one	their	yours
H	nobody	theirs	yourself
he	none	them	
her	nothing	themselves	
hers		these	
herself		they	
him		this	
himself		those	
his			

WORD BANKS Punctuation

Apostrophe

An apostrophe can show ownership or missing letters (it is – it's). For ownership, the rules are:

Singular owners add: **'s**.

Plural owners not ending in 's' add: **'s**.

Plural owners ending in 's', add: **s'**.

➾ The monkey snapped my car**'s** antenna and stabbed me with it.

( ) Brackets

Brackets contain a piece of additional information put into the main sentence. We can also use commas to do this job.

➾ The baby **(**when he is hungry**)** will bite my finger.

: Colon

A colon introduces more information. This information may be a list or a second clause adding information to the first clause.

➾ These animals are not edible**:** camels, kangaroos and parrots.

, Comma

A comma separates parts of a sentence and can be similar to a pause in speech.

➾ Although nobody is looking at him**,** the panda is still hiding in the corner.

— Dash

A dash is used in informal writing.

➾ That hat looks great**—**everyone will love it.

... Ellipsis

Ellipsis is the name for three dots that show the writing is incomplete.

➾ The lion leapt towards the unsuspecting visitor and before you knew it **...**

10. Apostrophes

Apostrophes have two functions: to show contractions (**I won't**) and possession (**Shakespeare's tragedy**). They are not used to show the plural of a noun.

My novel's on dinosaurs contain numerous inaccuracies.	My novels on dinosaurs contain numerous inaccuracies. ✔
For now, the terrorists threats have not cowed the community.	For now, the terrorists' threats have not cowed the community. ✔

9. Nouns ending in y

Nouns ending in **y** often produce similar confusion with regard to possession. If you want to talk about something belonging to a country, for instance, write **country's**, not **countries**.

8. Conjunction confusion

Conjunctions like *and*, *but* and *for* join principal clauses. Students often use *however*, *therefore*, and *thus* as if they were conjunctions, but they are not. They're adverbs, and can't connect principal clauses—you'll still need a semicolon or full stop.

I studied for hours but he never opened a book—and we both topped the exam.	I studied for hours but he never opened a book yet we both topped the exam. ✔

It's usually more graceful, however, to place *however*, *therefore*, and similar words not right at the beginning but at some convenient pause later on:

Truth is a good thing; it is not, however, the highest political good.

7. Infamy and notoriety

Infamous is not a fancy way of saying famous. It means the opposite: famously wicked or bad. Gandhi was famous; Hitler was infamous. Likewise, *notoriety* doesn't mean just being widely known—it means being known for being bad.

Although cryogenics was introduced over a decade ago, it is only now receiving the notoriety it deserves.	Although cryogenics was introduced over a decade ago, it is only now receiving the attention it deserves. ✔

6. Practice and practise

In many English-speaking countries (UK, Australia, India and Canada) **practice** is the noun, **practise** the verb. However, in the US the spelling **practice** is more often used for both the noun and the verb.

You need to practise your English..	You need to practice your English.. ✔

5. Advice and advise

Advice is a noun and advise is the verb form and you clearly have to use the noun before the adjective.

She gave me very good advise on buying a car.	She gave me very good advice on buying a car. ✔

4. Intents and purposes

Not intensive purposes.

For all intensive purposes, Apple has won the computer wars.	For all intents and purposes, Apple has won the phone wars. ✔

3. Of or Off

People often use these words interchangeably, but each has its own correct usage. It helps to think of it like this: ***Of*** implies belonging to something or coming from. ***Off*** implies to be removed, away from or less. **Dispose of** is an exception.

The car went of the road.	The car went off the road. ✔

2. Principal/principle

Principal is an adjective meaning **foremost** or **most important**, while principle is a noun meaning **guiding idea.**

The Constitution of India lays down the fundamental principal and rights of citizens.	The Constitution of India lays down the fundamental principle and rights of citizens. ✔

1. It's/its

Because apostrophes are used for possession as well as contraction, many students get confused about the distinction between them. Remember that **it's** is a contraction, not a possessive: *It's = it is*. *It*, like other pronouns (*he, his; she, her*) doesn't take an apostrophe to show possession:

The baby howled when I stole it's toy.	The baby howled when I stole its toy. ✔

Who's and *whose* have the same distinction. *Who's* is a contraction of **who is** or, less commonly, **who has. Whose** is the possessive of **who.**

Whose ready to go out tonight?	Who's ready to go out tonight? ✔

WORD BANKS Homographs

words that are identical with another in spelling but different in meaning.

angle
arms
back
ball
bank
bar
bark
base
bat
bay
beam
bear
beat
bill
bit
blind
block
blow
board
booty
bow
brand
cape
case
cast
change
charge
chop
club
coach
coat
coast
cold
column
corn
count
court
craft
crane
cricket
crop
cross
crow
dock
down
draught
draw
drill
drive
drone
duck
express
fair
fast
felt
file
fill
fine
fire
fit
flag
fleet
float
fold
foot
form
game
gape
grain
grate
grave
ground
gum
hail
hamper
hand
hide
hit
hold
host
iron
jam
jar
joint
jumper
June
just
kid
kind
kite
lap
last
lay
lead
lean
leaves
left
let
letter
lie
lift
light
line
list
litter
lock
log
mail
march
mass
master
match
may
mean
might
mine
mint
mould
mount
nail
nature
note
order
organ
page
palm
pass
patient
peal
plot
plug
pole
port
post
pound
power
private
prune
pupil
race
range
rank
record
rent
rest
rifle
right
ring
rock
roll
rose
round
row
ruler
rung
sack
safe
save
scale
scales
seal
season
shed
sheet
sign
sink
smoke
soil
sound
sow
speaker
spell
spoke
spring
squash
staff
stage
stall
stand
star
state
steer
stern
stick
stock
stole
strike
stud
stump
suit
swallow
swift
table
tear
temper
tile
till
top
train
trip
tumbler
turn
vote
wake
watch
wave
well
wind
work
yawn

WORD BANKS Homophones

ail / ale
air / heir
aisle / isle / I'll
allowed / aloud
alter / altar
arc / ark
arms / alms
ascent / assent
ate / eight
aunt / aren't
awe / or / oar / ore
bail / bale
bald / bawled
bare / bear
bark / barque
barren / baron
base / bass
be / bee
beach / beech
been / bean
beer / bier
bell / belle
berry / bury
birth / berth
bite / bight
blew / blue
boar / bore
board / bored
boarder / border
bold / bowled
born / borne
bough / bow
bow / beau
boy / buoy
braid / brayed
braise / brays
brake / break
bread / bred
brews / bruise
bridal / bridle
but / butt
buy / by / bye
cannon / canon

canvas / canvass
capital / capitol
carrot / carat
cast / caste
caw / core / corps
cede / seed
ceiling / sealing
cellar / seller
cent / scent / sent
centred / scented
cents / scents / sense
cereal / serial
cheap / cheep
check / cheque
chews / choose
choral / coral
cite / sight / site
clause / claws
coarse / course
coat / cote
colonel / kernel
council / counsel
creak / creek
crews / cruise
cue / queue
curb / kerb
currant / current
cygnet / signet
days / daze
dear / deer
dew / due
die / dye
died / dyed
dies / dyes
doe / dough
draft / draught
draw / drawer
dying / dyeing
earn / urn
ewe / you / yew
ewes / use
eye / I
eyelet / islet

faint / feint
fair / fare
farther / father
fate / fete
feat / feet
find / fined
fir / fur
flaw / floor
flea / flee
flew / flu / flue
flocks / phlox
flow / floe
flower / flour
for / fore / four
fort / fought
foul / fowl
frays / phrase
freeze / frieze
gait / gate
gamble / gambol
genes / jeans
gild / guild
gnaw / nor
gored / gourd
gorilla / guerrilla
grate / great
grater / greater
groan / grown
guest / guessed
hail / hale
hanger / hangar
hart / heart
heal / heel / he'll
hear / here
heard / herd
hears / here's
hew / hue
higher / hire
him / hymn
ho / hoe
hoard / horde
hoarse / horse
hose / hoes

hole / whole
holy / wholly
hour / our
idle / idol
in / inn
island / Ireland
jam / jamb
key / quay
knave / nave
knead / need / kneed
knew / new
knight / night
knot / not
know / no
knows / nose
lacks / lax
lain / lane
laps / lapse
larva / lava
lead / led
leak / leek
lessen / lesson
liar / lyre
licence / license
lieu / loo / Lou
lightening / lightning
links / lynx
load / lode
loan / lone
loot / lute
made / maid
mail / male
main / mane
maize / maze
mall / maul
manner / manor
mantel / mantle
mare / mayor
marshal / martial
meat / meet / mete
medal / meddle
metal / mettle
metre / meter

Evaluation Sheet

Name: ____________________

Date: ____________________

Criterion	Superior	Satisfactory	Meets requirements	Unsatisfactory
Each assignment conveys a clear and specific purpose				
The student selects facts and composes genres that fit with his or her overall purpose and framing context				
The student successfully identifies and employs the conventions of each chosen genre				
The student places and organises his or her arguments logically				
The student shows connections between different points to support and develop his or her ideas				
The student demonstrates his or her ability to research, select and integrate sources				
The student offers sufficient evidence and explanation to develop his or her main ideas in each genre				

This sheet evaluates the student's writing skills.

Notes: